DOVES IN THE RAT RACE

DOVES IN THE RAT RACE

Christian Life-Style Today

TERENCE COPLEY

EPWORTH PRESS

All rights reserved. No part of this publication may be reproduced, stored in a retrieval system, or transmitted, in any form or by any means, electronic, mechanical, photocopying, recording or otherwise, without the prior permission of the publishers, Epworth Press.

Copyright © Terence Copley 1989

0 7162 0458 4

First published 1989
by Epworth Press
Room 195, 1 Central Buildings, Westminster
London SW1H 9NR

Photoset by J&L Composition Ltd, Filey, North Yorkshire
and printed in Great Britain by
Richard Clay Ltd, Bungay, Suffolk

Contents

Preface	vii
Part One What Makes a Christian?	1
Part Two Christian Beliefs	19
1 About God	21
2 About Jesus	30
3 About the Bible	40
4 About the Next World	51
Part Three Christian Behaviour	59
1 The Moral Image: Sex and Loving	61
2 At Home	70
3 In the World	77
4 Trying to Bring About a Better World	88
Part Four Christians Together	95
1 At Worship	97
2 The Church	103
Acknowledgments	111

Preface

This book is about what it means to be a Christian. Like most books it is biased, because it is written from a point of view. I have to be agnostic or atheistic or religious or from a specific religion. It happens that I am a Christian, of the sort that could jokingly be described as card-carrying. That is, I belong to a Christian group; I take part in worship; I attempt to live by 'Christian principles', whatever they may be. But I am not claiming to be holier than thou (or you!), however different your understanding of the Christian faith may be and whether you feel that you belong to it or not. There is just as much chance that your interpretation of Christianity might be as right as mine, or we may both be right, or both wrong. Who is to say? Indeed, one of the central themes of the book is that the strength and weakness of Christianity simultaneously is that no one can lay down for you a precise life-plan or set of rules and in many ways the Christian life is what we make it. The Bible, churches, Christian literature and Christian leaders may give good advice, but none of them can do it for us. We have to work out what it means in our job, on our street, in our family life, in our century.

Doves in the Rat Race

Because of this, the whole thing has become confused, so that many people aren't sure what it means to be a Christian any more.

'You can be a Christian without going to church.'

'A Christian is any good person.'

'There's no noticeable difference between a good Christian and a good atheist.'

'A Christian has to be born again.'

These are just some of the phrases that are bandied about. Many people are sympathetic to Christianity and would be indignant if it were said that because they have no church link they aren't Christian; many people go to church occasionally – Christmas, Easter, harvest, perhaps; some go regularly to worship. Does it matter?

This book is written to try to clarify what it means in belief and behaviour to be a Christian and in so doing perhaps to help other Christians, for if Christianity has any value at all it must mean something.

The book is also intended for others who feel themselves to be sympathetically on the fringe but wouldn't go so far as to label themselves 'Christian', and for those who are bewildered but would like to know more, and even for the frankly sceptical. It is not its aim to produce Christians, but if it can dispel some of the fudge that has come to surround Christianity in our Western culture it will have succeeded. For Christianity in our culture is not threatened nearly so much by atheism as by vagueness and well-meant but misunderstanding

Preface

lip service. So many people perceive it as 'a good thing'. But in what way? It seems to make no practical difference. Sure there must be more to it than that. Does it boil down to an observable set of beliefs or a clear pattern of behaviour? Or both? Or does it not 'boil down' to anything a single sentence can sum up? Is it a more subtle and pervasive attitude towards life? This book is about my answers to these questions. I hope you find yours.

Dawlish, 1989　　　　　　　　　　　　Terence Copley

PART ONE
What Makes a Christian?

The most dangerous people are those who claim that on any major issues – politics, education, religion or whatever – they have no prejudice. Such people are dangerous because they cannot see where their prejudices lie. For we all have prejudices built upon the basis of all sorts of irrational impressions and associations and of course on the firm foundation of the prejudice of others. It is commonly said, 'I have firmly held opinions and beliefs, but you have prejudices.' There is truth in that!

Take, for instance, someone as well known as the Prime Minister. By virtue of radio, television, newspapers, magazines and the vast amount of coverage they extend to the famous, we have all been fed a picture of the PM. We feel that we know the PM just as well, if not better, than we know many of the people who live round about us and whom we meet perhaps daily. We certainly claim to know whether we like or dislike the PM and we can get very heated in discussion with those who take, very unreasonably, the opposite view. The

Doves in the Rat Race

truth is that we hardly know the PM at all. Not only are we being fed what the PM's public relations people want us to see, but we are being fed through the eyes of the media, some of whom have their own axe to grind for or against the PM. Anyway the PM has the right to expect some sort of private life, even in high office, and the closure of this door leaving us on the outside shuts off the biggest insight into the real PM. This leaves us with glimpses and impressions which could be severely misleading. I need hardly point out that this applies to whatever PM or party is in power.

In a surprising way there is for many people a direct parallel here with their view of Christianity. Rarely will it be based on careful thought or on an attempt rationally to understand the nature of the faith. Discussion and thought may be bottom of the agenda that leads to our stance on religion. Much more common will be a haphazard collection of attitudes and impressions, some derived from our personal experience and some derived from our encounters with others, especially our parents and close friends.

I wonder why so many people seem to be surprised that our basic attitude to faith owes so much to the attitude of our parents. We may never grow up into our own beliefs and away from them. For instance where parents view religion as of no practical importance, so that it is never discussed in the home and the children never have any contact with a place of worship, it can hardly be wondered at that a deep and fundamental attitude is transmitted

What Makes a Christian?

that religion is not worth bothering about, and that so often the lives of the children from parents such as these will reflect the same values. Sheer prejudice!

Or again, the parent who, having beliefs, decides not to take or send the children to church but to leave them until they're old enough to make up their own minds, passes on the mighty impression that if you can live happily without religion until you're sixteen you can presumably go on like this till you're eighty and so you never feel the need to bother to make up your own mind on these matters at all. Such abdication by the parents will in practice condition the child's response. It will be one of respectful agnosticism or practical atheism.

Similarly, how often in conversation we can find ourselves talking to adults wounded by some childhood experience of churchgoing. They found Sunday School boring or they didn't like the vicar and they go on quite happy to live by these childhood prejudices into adult life and death. What flimsy evidence it all is!

But there are other assumptions, too, from which people derive or strengthen their prejudices. One of these is that religion has been disproved by science. Who is actually saying this and on what evidence? Many people believe that the debate is over between these two giants when, at an intellectual level, it may scarcely have begun. Of course belief in evolution cannot be reconciled with a literal reading of the Bible, but this need not be upsetting to Christians, as we shall see later. It is an interesting possibility that for some, faith in science

Doves in the Rat Race

has replaced faith in religion. In either case blind faith can be very dangerous.

Again, some people reinforce their prejudice against Christianity by pointing out another widespread belief, namely that the churches are getting emptier and that, presumably, if the line on the graph continues down, there will be no Christianity left by a predictable year. Better get out now, and leave it to the old and those who need it as a crutch. Again, one has to ask rigorously, who is saying this and on what evidence? For the main trend of evidence seems to be pointing to continuing growth in Christianity when we look on a world basis, even if the UK statistic has shown some dips this century.

When we start to question these assumptions all sorts of other important questions arise anyway. The sales of religious books are increasing, but how does one interpret that? Some churches are gaining ground fast, even in the UK. And do numbers matter anyway, or shouldn't we be looking at truth claims, for after all it shouldn't matter to me whether there are one million, fifty million or one hundred million Christians in the world. The question should be: is the Christian faith true and is it worth bothering with?

Other people can be found who will tell us that the reason why they have distanced themselves from Christianity is that they have met so many people who practise it who are hypocritical and don't live up to it. What a bad example they set. I couldn't be part of that rotten apple etc. It is always

What Makes a Christian?

interesting to meet such morally superior people – or perhaps they were never told that Christianity is for sinners and that Jesus, who can so easily be turned by our magic into a white, middle-class Westerner, concerned with respectability and the protection of property, himself befriended notorious promiscuous people, collaborators with an occupying power, the poor and at least one terrorist or ex-terrorist. He is the Simon, not Simon Peter, of Mark 3.18 and other references, variously translated Simon the Zealot, Simon the Patriot etc. The zealots were intent on pushing the occupying Romans out of the holy land by force if necessary. I wonder who Jesus' friends would be in our time. That isn't to say he defended the actions of his friends, but he remained their good and trusted friend. Maybe we should be ruder to people who would be Christians if it wasn't for those of us who are! They don't seem to have grasped much of it.

Other people will hesitate about Christianity because they've been fed the idea that you have to accept all of it, or none of it. You must believe all the Bible or none. If you can't accept one point of doctrine or one Bible account you should, if you're honest, resign, they imagine. How far from the truth this is! If you join a political party you are not committed to supporting their every move. A study of backbenchers is sufficient to disprove that! You join because you commit yourself in general to their approach and philosophy, not because you are prepared to back them right or wrong to the

Doves in the Rat Race

suppression of your conscience. Christianity is no different. Indeed, careful study of Christian history shows that at many times the reform or advance of the faith has been advanced by rebels who, led by their conscience and a rediscovery of some biblical emphasis or other, campaigned against the orthodoxy of their time.

There are other prejudices about Christianity that may have come from primary school, where sometimes an unthinking approach to RE sows seeds of later scepticism. To be told, without any comment, about the God of the flood or the God of the plagues may plant in the minds of children a fundamentally unpleasant concept of God that may feed adolescent rejection and scepticism. Even Father Christmas, who corresponds to so much of what small children are told about God – he is kindly, remote, magic, loves children, a father figure – can contribute to subconscious rejection of God. For when Santa has been unveiled as a well-meant adult ploy, what does this do to God? Have they invented him to fool us, or make us good, or cheer us up? Or, worse, have they even fooled themselves? We have to be so careful in what we say to small children!

I am not aiming, in a few pages, to dispose of, or in modern parlance, rubbish the case against Christianity. But I am trying to make a major and often over-looked point: the rejection of Christianity by many people in our time has nothing to do with intellectual arguments and the rise of atheism. These are important, but they are not the real battle

What Makes a Christian?

ground. Indeed the intellectual arguments for believers and unbelievers alike may just be clever ways whereby educated people can argue their prejudices, clothed in fine words. The reason why people have turned away from the Christian faith is wrapped up in the sorts of assumptions and prejudices I have been listing in that great coercive power of our time, fashion. Moreover careful questioning reveals that they may not have in fact turned away at all. It could simply be that the possibility of honest, serious commitment to Christianity has never been put to them. That may be because they are imprisoned by these assumptions of upbringing or it may be because the churches have failed to grasp what is really going on in such a way as to be able to challenge it. Real mission isn't about running up to people in the street to ask them if they've heard about Jesus. It must begin with Christians themselves looking very carefully at their faith, how they are communicating it and how it relates to trends good and bad in society today. Only when we begin to be clear on these issues can we begin to make sense to outsiders.

Christians and non–Christians alike share common problems. These include: coping with the pressures of adolescence; life with a partner; life without a partner, perhaps via bereavement or divorce; coping with career; 'mid-life' crises; the failures that occur in everyone's life at some time. Infantile Christianity, the Christianity bred on the sorts of misinformation discussed above, cannot

Doves in the Rat Race

help people here, but adult Christianity can. Many people would genuinely like to be Christian, but need to be told that doubt is part of honest faith, not an enemy. It is not necessary to know all the answers to be truly Christian. You don't have to go back to the infant stage of belief to be a Christian. But you do have to see some of the prejudices and assumptions of our time and how they are at work on us in order, as it were, to rise above them.

The sceptic will still point out that many people appear to lead happy and fulfilled lives all around us without any reference to religion or the supernatural. This is true, to a point, but as an argument is a bit like the 'Would Harold have won at Hastings if he'd had machine guns?' type. We cannot know. Would the lives of religionless people have been happier with religion? We cannot know either. We can say that the rejection of religion, in its widest sense, is a recent and Western phenomenon in the history of the human species. A drop in the ocean of mankind, a few of whom have arrogated to themselves the ability to see through and dispense with a dimension of life which for thousands of years and in thousands of cultures has offered enrichment. They could, of course, be right. They could have seen through and demolished it. Only time will prove or disprove that. But on the patterns of human happiness imposed by the Western world on the rest of the world during this century – wars, the arms race, the failure to deal with illiteracy, poverty and starvation in the rest of the world, the failure to handle conservation, the

What Makes a Christian?

destruction in our century of the world environment, the dreaming up and carrying out of the purposes of Auschwitz, Belsen and the nauseating rest – none of these gives me confidence that the attempt to bury religion in our culture has been entirely beneficial, to us or to others.

Perhaps the time has come, for us as individuals and as a society, to challenge the assumptions implicit in our culture, into which we were born and reared, assumptions that are partly common to all of us, both religious and non-religious people. We assume that life is forever, and focus on the here and now. So people don't die any more; they pass away, usually when we aren't looking. What matters is my enjoyment, so I 'need' more money; I can then enjoy myself more. A 'good' job means a well-paid job, with good 'prospects', i.e. of more money and promotion. My standard of living should keep on rising. It doesn't matter what I do, as long as I don't 'hurt' anybody, though by this we usually mean physically. After all, only my emotional feelings matter, you will get over your snivelling. People who steal or damage property must be dealt with severely, but promiscuity and adultery don't matter, provided you don't give me AIDS. These seem to be some of the unquestioned values of our times. The condom adverts play on our fear of AIDS but assume without question sexual intercourse within courtship. So along with warnings which are spelt out are passed values which aren't, the 'condom culture' as it has been called. The Christian is caught up in some of these

Doves in the Rat Race

traps because like everyone else the Christian grows up in the surrounding culture and absorbs these values with the air that is breathed in.

Perhaps this leads on to the question: who or what is a Christian? For while most people could answer yes or no to the question 'Are you a Christian?', they would be much more hard put to define what a Christian is. Perhaps that is because it has become so confused with the fashions and values of our time. For another assumption many people have is that a Christian is distinguishable only by beliefs, about God, Jesus, the church etc. rather than by behaviour, in a particular set of moral values or approach to life. Again, this puts people off. For in the end, they're not looking for a set of beliefs about the universe, but for a way of life which is refreshing and honest. At the same time we have to acknowledge that some people aren't looking for anything! Perhaps that is sad.

So what is Christianity? The immediate response of some to this question is to answer that a Christian is a good living person. This strange view has arisen perhaps because Christianity has become so identified with our culture that people find it impossible to distinguish the two, so that any one who is living 'a good life' as it has become known, is identified by some with upholding Christian values. Clearly we would not want to define a Christian as a bad living person, but the question arises as to whether the idea that a Christian is a good person goes nearly far enough, and yet in some ways goes too far. For under the heading

What Makes a Christian?

good living person would undoubtedly come many thousands, millions of Muslims, Sikhs, Hindus, Jews, Buddhists and atheists. It would seem to help neither them nor Christians to bracket them altogether as if they were members of one big, happy Christian family. Indeed, many of them would find it quite insulting to be labelled like that. The other problem in the idea that a Christian is any good living person is that in practice this is conceived of in such a negative way: to be 'good' you have to not commit murder, or steal or rape, the sort of 'goodness' most of us can manage quite easily and which claims to be based on the Ten Commandments. If this is so, it's a fairly selective reading of them, because most of us do not keep the sabbath (Saturday) holy and the one on adultery is regarded as optional by some, if behaviour is the standard of judgment. Moreover this 'goodness' view of Christianity omits to take into account Jesus' strong advice to one of the 'best' people he ever met (Mark 10.17–22), advice that although he was good in all these ways he was not good enough. This young man who asked Jesus sincerely what he had to do to inherit eternal life, when he was leading an exemplary life already, was clinging to one worldly value he would not let go. In his case it was money. The view that a Christian is merely a good person manages to omit any link between Christianity and Jesus himself; it's really a sort of I-anity rather than Christianity. Jesus doesn't seem much to do with it.

A different view is asserted by those who regard

Doves in the Rat Race

Christianity as a set of beliefs, concerned with fairly remote matters like the origins of the universe, the existence of God and the specialness of Jesus. Such beliefs are held with some sincerity by proponents of this view, though they never quite manage to introduce a contact point into their daily life, except perhaps to roll up to church for the carol service, the harvest festival and perhaps Easter. You may still have your children 'done' (infant baptism) but the every week church attenders are viewed with some reserve as fanatics – that's taking things a bit far, for after all 'we can worship God just as well in the beauty of the countryside during a spin in the car on Sunday as in a church . . .' While this view is theologically quite possible and defensible, one wonders how many of the people who are heard to say it actually bother to do the worship bit when they go out in the car.

My view is that the reality of Christianity, or what is possible to Christians, lies in a sort of amalgam of these two views, but with a big difference too. It is about beliefs, and it is about behaviour, both bound together. This is what the Bible calls 'faith' and 'works'. One without the other is less than the Christian life. It is about a re-ordering of our perspectives on life in such a way that our daily life is very much affected, not in the obtrusive way which is characteristic of the religious maniac or the very insecure believer, but in a deep and quiet and real way. Whatever words we use to describe him, Christ will be at the centre, the best window into God we can see. As

What Makes a Christian?

Christians 'We place our destiny in the hands of the Lord, not in the hands of men, because his mercy is as great as his majesty' (Sirach 2.18). In other words, we acknowledge the boss, not as a tyrant dictator but as a personality both friendly and also to whom we are accountable.

Some people appear to become Christians suddenly and can place date, time and circumstances clearly. Acts 9 suggests that Saul becoming a Christian was an experience of this sort. This type of experience can also put off outsiders who may feel guilty because they haven't had something of that sort, or feel that the absence of such an experience is proof that they are not yet Christian or fully Christian. This would be a pity, for while church history can produce many case studies of dramatic and sudden, or apparently sudden, conversions, it can produce hundreds times more experiences of people who found that over a period of time Christianity grew on them, or in them, until one day they realized that the Christianity they were professing had really become theirs, no longer the faith of their parents or culture or upbringing, but the faith they had nurtured or that had mysteriously grown inside them until it had become their own, with the help of what early Quakers used to call 'the Seed Christ' inside them.

This book aims to explore the Christian way of life, not by or for professional theologians, not even by a professional Christian in the sense of someone ordained to the full-time work of the church, but hopefully in ordinary words and

Doves in the Rat Race

avoiding at least some of the jargon which can be so off-putting in any religion or denomination. In-groups always generate their own language which tries to describe their experience. It's fine if you're in the group, share the experience and the language helps to bridge the gap. But to the outsider looking in, the jargon has no currency. For many people in-phrases like 'being saved', 'sacrifice', 'redemption', 'justification', even 'died for you' in reference to a death 2000 years ago, mean very little now. Christians have to learn to reach out with new words and to listen to the questions and experience of outsiders, who may not yet be Christian but are already, to lapse into jargonese, 'children of God' or subject to God's concern.

Words are themselves images, just as statues are. It is the reality that they try to describe that matters. It would be just as much a mistake to worship a word image as to worship a stone one. No one word or phrase can be insisted on as only or always true. In the first place words can never fully describe experiences and in the second place words change their meaning. When that happens we have to trade them in for new ones. There is continuity even now between modern Greek and the Greek of the New Testament bridging a 2000-year gap, but there are massive differences of vocabulary, of grammar, of idiom and – most important – the host culture of the language has changed. It is the same for any language. Who now in English readily understands their trespasses being forgiven?

Christian belief and behaviour is a response to a

What Makes a Christian?

reality that the words barely describe, the reality of God in action. This reality is always greater than the words. Sometimes the words can put people off and the reality fails to penetrate through them, where in another generation or place, it once did. When this happens religion has become a prisoner of its own language. Yet we can only use words (and paint or music, which can sometimes present truth as well as preachers can, though like words pictures and music can date). Words will have more or less meaning as they reach, or fail to reach, our experience. The only way to explore Christian lifestyle is to look at aspects of Christian belief and aspects of Christian behaviour in more detail. That is the concern of the rest of this book.

It is written of Abraham that he set out, not knowing where he was going, but in the belief that God would be with him – beliefs and behaviour together again! (Gen. 12). In a way that can become a model for the nature of Christianity, which is after all the child of Abraham's Judaism. No one hands us Christianity on a plate. No one can tell us what to believe or do our believing for us. No one can tell us in detail how to live or live our lives for us. Our existence is not ordered by rules such as the Muslim prayer rituals or the Jewish dietary requirements or the Sikh dress regulations, which all play a part in these faiths. Christianity doesn't come in a pre-packaged unit like the how-to-speak-a-foreign-language cassette and book or the car repair manual. The Bible isn't that sort of book. Christianity is always a DIY job. You learn as you go

Doves in the Rat Race

along and you make painful mistakes. But it's the DIY nature that makes it so interesting – and that is always more satisfying than the package approach!

PART TWO
Christian Beliefs

1 · ABOUT GOD

All about God in a few pages! 'God' is one of the smallest words in the English language yet it covers one of the deepest realities and produces the strongest feelings, for and against. It is the incapability of religious believers to prove that there is a God that is used most readily by unbelievers to bolster their confidence that they've dispensed with the whole thing as mature adults. But the other side of this must not be forgotten either; while it has never been possible to prove God's existence in such a way as to demonstrate beyond all doubt to all thinking people that God is there, it is equally impossible to demonstrate beyond all doubt that God is not there. Touché! So we must in our search as Christians or as interested outsiders be willing to surrender proof and disproof at the beginning. This shouldn't worry us too much, for in reality many of the major things in our lives are based on a faith that bears no proof. We believe in love and hence relate to another person and perhaps marry; but it will never be proved beyond doubt that we acted simply out of 'love', however that is defined, or

Doves in the Rat Race

that the partner we chose was necessarily the only or best suited partner for us. The same can be said of career; any of us might have excelled far more in another field than the one we chose, but we shall never know. Our unproveable faith is that the job choice we made was the best, or at least the best at the time, and we accept a working life based on that. We also believe in justice and from earliest childhood have a strong sense of it. Look how we burn with anger, perhaps for months or even years, when as children we were punished for something we didn't do. The teacher who wants to attract undying hatred from the class keeps them all in because someone has misbehaved and won't own up. But what is this justice we believe in and is it more than my own self-interest or the self-interest of the community of which I am a part? It is possible to cast doubts on the nature of justice, loyalty, love, patriotism or any other unproveable quality, if we try hard enough. So we have to be careful not to get paranoid about God merely because he (or she, for even these words are pictures not definitions) can't be proved.

The reality is more complex, for the reality is that our belief or disbelief in God varies according to the circumstances in which we find ourselves. Imagine for a moment that you are in an aeroplane flying to your holiday destination and a voice comes over the PA system: 'Good morning, passengers. This is your captain speaking. It is a fine sunny morning, flying conditions are perfect and we are at 50,000 feet. But I regret to inform

Christian Beliefs

you that the engines have just fallen off and we shall very shortly be landing.' The plane then goes into a steep dive ...

In these circumstances many of those passengers would find within themselves submerged beliefs and a capacity to pray and to pray quickly that, in the comfortable airport lounge, they didn't know they had, or even scoffed at in others. It is easy to mock this sort of faith as emergency insurance, pie in the sky when you die as it is caustically called. That isn't entirely fair. It could be that our cosy day-to-day existence, for many of us spent inside buildings, is within an artificial environment that we control whereas we don't entirely control the outside world, the storms, the elements, the planet. Even our body's health is not guaranteed. Air-conditioned, centrally-heated buildings may enhance our illusion of our own invulnerability and immortality. The fact is we are vulnerable, emotionally and physically and we will all die one day. Deep within us we know that, but we like to shut it out. So the passenger in my improbable aircraft scenario is the one who really has his feet on the ground. It is we who are living in cloud-cuckoo land below.

Within the unbeliever, then, is residual belief, just as within the believer there is residual doubt. I have met a few believers who seemed on the surface certain. They knew they were destined for heaven, it was as clear as their face. Maybe ... Such people are sometimes hard to live with because you can't tell them anything. They know the answers

Doves in the Rat Race

already. But I doubt whether they are that sure all the time, and they will be fortunate indeed if they are not, in the words of the Lord's Prayer, put to the test one day. Jesus was never that sure, not for twenty-four hours of every day. On the cross, under the extremity of isolation, humiliation and pain he felt forsaken by God (Mark 14.34).

So belief and disbelief have in common that they both include doubt and they both vary in intensity. Doubt should not be seen by Christians as a dirty word, something about which they should feel guilty and seek to repress or cast out. Doubt is simply honesty in action, asking questions, accepting that faith has to grow and change as we grow and change or else it fossilizes, like the infant school faith which is like a snake skin. We all crawl out of it but some of us never replace it. Doubt is recognizing that, intellectually speaking, we could be wrong, that there are other interpretations of human experience than the belief we have or have not chosen. It is doubt and honesty that compel us to recognize that at times the honest Christian is almost an atheist and that the honest atheist is almost a believer.

Yet at a deeper, emotional level, many people feel a seeking, a longing, a wish to believe. Christians have been reluctant to deal with this wish, because since Freud and Marx it has been unfashionable to admit to it. Just as Marks and Spencer transformed retailing, Marx and Freud transformed Western psychology! The thrust of what they did was to discredit such longings as

Christian Beliefs

fantasy, as wishful thinking, the quest for security, as an unworthy basis on which the parasite of religion fastened to enslave the hearts and minds of people. Intellectually this interpretation could of course be right. The small child's longing for Father Christmas doesn't mean that there is a Father Christmas, though as adults we have to be careful not to write Father Christmas off in shallow disbelief. What I mean is that while no adult would assert his physical existence, as a picture way of embodying what to us may be the spirit of Christmas – joviality, giving, etc. – Father Christmas is 'real'. He is certainly 'real' in cash terms, as he fills the shop tills with money from October to December each year and his cash value can be assessed!

Just as what we long for is not real simply because we long for it, it is not unreal either on account of our longing for it. God is not unreal just because people want to believe in him, because many of them find it fulfilling and helpful. Certainly we can live without a God who is a distant caretaker, an old man with a long beard on a throne in the sky, but if we locate God in the here and now, deep within people and their hopes and fears rather than as an interplanetary figure, he is not an unworthy figure. On its own, of course, that does not prove anything.

The difficulty is, we talk and argue about 'God' and yet so often people mean different things when they use the word. It would have been better to discuss their idea of what God was or wasn't first.

Doves in the Rat Race

For do any Christians really believe that God is this old man on his throne in the sky? Yet this is what many atheists feel Christians are saying.

Where are we to start in the maze of seeking not only a meaning for 'God', but some sort of idea or concept or experience that can somehow be communicated to those who feel they haven't seen it or that it isn't there to see? Jesus' understanding can help. Jesus was a Jew, and although modern Christianity has largely lost touch with its Jewish roots and parents, the search for God could well benefit from looking at Jewish views and at the views of Jesus himself. We may safely rid ourselves of the camels and sandals view of the Bible because although the technology of Bible times was not as developed as ours, their brains were and they were perfectly capable of thinking through these knottier problems of life. True, they may not have invented the automatic washer and liberated people from drudgery but they hadn't invented high capacity bombs or destroyed the rain forests either, so it makes us about quits for use of intelligence.

Whereas the ancient Greeks thought in many ways like us, or as we should more humbly say, we think in many ways like them, and most of the 'modern' ideas used in discussing God were old in ancient Greece, the Hebrews had developed differently. They had few, if any, abstract words in their language, so they were spared all the difficulties we face when we start on terms and definitions. And they had an inbuilt sense of seeing through a symbol to the reality behind it. They

Christian Beliefs

didn't expect to take every word literally, as we in a technological age do. That's why they could write poetry like the psalms or talk of God's bowels being moved as a way of describing his extreme and costly concern for his people. Yet they were aware of God's distance, of his majesty. The strange idea among some Protestant Christians that God belongs to them, that he is their God, that Jesus is their Jesus, that somehow we've got him on our side, in our pocket, that we're pulling the strings, was quite foreign to the people of the Bible. For the nation that was capable of the belief that they were the chosen people was capable also of seeing that God would, metaphorically speaking, wallop them if they were bad or raise up a new people for himself if it suited his purpose. No tame God there! This warning, nearly threatening view of the God who doesn't belong to us, who is his own person ('I AM who I AM' or 'I WILL BE WHO I WILL BE' of Ex. 3.14) finds its place in the teaching of Jesus. Mark 13 has more threats than comfort and the story of the unforgiving servant in Matt. 18.21–35 doesn't exactly have a happily-ever-after ending. When Luke records some people tut-tutting over the fate of various of their countrymen and their implication that the people died because they were bad (the punishment view of disaster), he also records (in 13.5) Jesus' devastating reply. You'll end up like them if you don't repent! Many Western Christians ignore this side of God because it is rather uncomfortable. But it is a reminder about who owns God. We don't. He isn't our creature. Quite the reverse.

Doves in the Rat Race

The significant thing in Jesus' life, however, is that this sense of God's mystery and distance is balanced by a shocking emphasis on his knownness and closeness. He is the 'Daddy' which is the proper translation of the word 'Abba' (Mark 14.36, though English translations prefer the stiff Victorian 'Father'). He is the Father to whom Jesus so often refers, the one to whom Jesus listened in the long night prayers, the sustainer of Jesus through a hard and tiring ministry, and at the end the one who enabled him to forgive his executioners (Luke 23.34). For the Christian God is supremely the God who raised Jesus from the dead. He is not an abstract idea, capable of proof or disproof. He is not essentially the creator of the universe millions of years ago, who's effectively since disappeared. He is the life force itself still busy and active today. Although New Testament accounts of the resurrection vary, they are quite clear on one point: Jesus didn't raise himself from the dead. God did it. The life force was indestructible. Jesus' view was that the essence of this life force was love and that we can tap into this within ourselves. It is not an 'idea' but a living, creative energy, personalized, directed, on the move, already in us, but repressed very effectively by all of us at times and by some more than others! It is this power that can grow more or burst out unexpectedly in the lives of people. God is not a distant indifferent caretaker of the universe, nor an ever-watching ogre totting up our sins, but an active, directed and personal force or energy or power turning death to life, bad to

Christian Beliefs

good, comforting the afflicted, afflicting the comfortable and beginning each new situation afresh for each of us. Resurrection is neither just a distant event connected with Jesus nor just a pious hope for me at the crematorium. It can begin now and yet involve past and future as well.

It is strange that in the light of Christian emphasis on life and on rebirth, Western Christianity seems to concentrate more on the death of Jesus than on the resurrection. Stained glass windows, crucifixes and the preachers' common emphasis that 'Jesus died for us' rather than rose for us are examples of this. Of course, it depends what rose means, as we shall see later. I do not think this has to mean the resuscitation of a corpse who then reappeared again, though it might mean that. The essential is this: the way in which Jesus lived, taught, died and, however we describe the detail, was bounced back again made God more real to those he encountered. His best followers pass on this impression today and if we want to understand God we must talk to the devout, and maybe listen more than we talk. So it is essentially Christ-ianity and not just I-anity; it is a way of life, not just a set of interesting or antique ideas. In this sense it is still true that the Christian faith is caught rather than taught. This means that Jesus is very much at its centre and we need to blow away some cobwebs about him to understand it further.

2 · ABOUT JESUS

I once stood in the Church of the Nativity in Bethlehem with a group of school children and an Orthodox (strict) Jewess as a guide. This church marks, according to tradition or legend, whichever you want to call it, the site of Jesus' birth and in a sort of cellar basement you can touch the metal star that marks the very spot where in that stable or cave, so long ago, it all happened. Well, that's what they tell you anyhow. I went there frankly sceptical about the chances of anyone remembering accurately something like that and feeling that the character of the stable or cave would anyhow be diminished by the church that so overwhelms the site. But as our guide was speaking, she began to talk to the children about the significance of Jesus' life, of his courage and dignity and of his love for God. As she was speaking she began to be so affected by what she was saying that she could no longer carry on and, choked up, appealed to me to help out. For the youngsters this was stunning, but for me more so. Here was an Orthodox Jewess, from a branch of Judaism that has traditionally

Christian Beliefs

viewed Jesus with suspicion, and certainly rejected the view that he could be the Messiah for Israel, so moved by his story that she couldn't carry on. I asked her about this afterwards.

'The trouble with you Christians,' she replied, 'is that you know too much about Jesus. You take him for granted. You fail to see what a great man he was. You've wrapped him up in doctrine ...'

I think she was right. In Western culture children are told about Jesus from such an early age that he's become part of their cultural background so that when they grow up and become us – adults! – it is quite impossible to stand back and appreciate Jesus like my Jewish friend could, looking in from the outside.

It isn't just that children think they know all about Jesus by the age of seven or so, it's that so often they've been told very complicated or adult bits about him too early. In the 1960s an educationalist called Ronald Goldman carried out a number of surveys into what primary school children were being told about Jesus at school or church or home. He concluded that they were being told ideas and concepts that were far too adult for them to understand, so creating in their minds the idea that Jesus was a magic figure, who could walk on water, turn it into wine and so on. When they reached the age of rejection of magic as something other than a clever adult illusion, they rejected Jesus also as a frankly impossible figure to believe in. Certainly some adolescents are so sceptical as to believe that Jesus never existed – people just aren't

Doves in the Rat Race

like him! But for all Goldman's researches, people were not deterred from telling unsuitable stories or passing on garbled ideas about Jesus and we may well find, if we were to repeat the survey in the 1990s, that Goldman's results are repeated. Plus ça change ...

Religious doctrine can also unwittingly overlay the man Jesus of Nazareth. It may be convenient for Christian tradition to walk the tightrope of maintaining the idea that Jesus was a God-man, but so often this is done at the expense of one aspect or the other and the more you lay on the God bit, the more the human bit disappears. If we are to have any understanding of Jesus at all it must begin from the point of his being a human being like the rest of us; this is something that can be grasped by atheists, agnostics, people of other faiths, small children, anyone. And it is fair to the records about Jesus that all testify that he was at the very least a human being. Of course most Christians would want to say more, some would want to say much more, but that is not a good starting point. That's a sort of commentary on the meaning of his life that faith might add afterwards. All this is not to say that he wasn't extraordinary, remarkable, unique, different in all sorts of ways from men and women of his time and perhaps of ours too, but it doesn't make the implications of his life the starting point.

To some extent this has always been vaguely recognized and children's Bibles and Christian literature have tried to produce a Jesus who can be

Christian Beliefs

understood by the young. Alas, the picture so often produced in practice is of a wimp. You see this white-skinned, white-robed, sad-faced man, wandering around, kissing babies, patting the elderly on the head, admiring wild flowers and telling people not to fight. It's a hard model to sell to boys in particular. Perhaps that's why they have become conditioned to rebel about going to church or Sunday School and why for many of them the macho image has no place for Jesus in it. What a travesty of New Testament evidence it all is! There Jesus is shown as a very determined character, who shows anger, e.g. Mark 3.5 when he was healing someone, and gets cross with his friends, e.g. Mark 10.14, when the disciples were trying to get rid of the children. He could also be quite scathing, e.g. Mark 7.6 and Matt. 23 when he attacked the Pharisees. He knew frustration as Mark 9.19 reveals when he faced crowds surrounding a violently ill boy. The more famous stories of Jesus' disruptive behaviour in the Temple in Mark 11 where he overturned the tables of the money changers, prevented the carriage of goods through the court and, according to the account in John 2, actually took a whip to them, is hardly meek and mild! So clearly children ought not to be fed the emasculated and wet picture of Jesus that has been peddled for too long.

The Victorians added their own bit to this image and because it has entered carols we happily perpetuate it every December.

Doves in the Rat Race

> And through all His wondrous childhood
> He would honour and obey,
> Love, and watch the lowly maiden
> In whose gentle arms he lay.
> Christian children all must be
> Mild, obedient, good as He.

This pallidly unattractive portrait exerts a continuing influence on some adults.

For others, the problem about Jesus is that they cannot distinguish him from a giant-sized version of the best in themselves. In other words, if asked to write about Jesus' personality they would start to describe an idealized version of all the things they admire: his truthfulness, courage or whatever. This is a bit like the manipulation of God described in the last section. Jesus in the end becomes the Jesus I want him to be and not the Jew Jesus of Nazareth who lived at a particular time and place in human history. I appeal to him to sanction what is in me. I use him as an image. Now this is the very sort of image the commandment warns us against.

Another major stumbling block about Jesus is the assertion which to many lies at the heart of Christian belief, that he is God's son. Some Christians would say that unless you can accept this you are not a Christian, thereby ruling out the Unitarians and other groups who have emphasized God's unity rather than the Father–Son–Holy Spirit Trinity. Neither view is without its problems, but for many the idea of Jesus as the Son of God is a stumbling block not so much of technical doctrine as basic understanding.

Christian Beliefs

Muslims and some Christian sympathizers have real difficulty with the idea that God needs or can have sons. It seems to compromise his Godness, his all-sufficiency, and over-humanizes him. Why can't he run the show himself? Surely he doesn't need a son. Is the virgin birth believable biology or any more satisfying as a religious idea? Then there's the problem of why God allowed his son to suffer, a conundrum that has exercised the minds of Christians for centuries. Can't be much of a Dad who'd let his son die. In the fourth century AD Christians debated the problem of the relationship of the Son to the Father with great passion. Various creeds emerged around that time in efforts to settle the dispute. The Nicene Creed said Jesus was

> The only Son of God,
> eternally begotten of the Father,
> God from God, Light from Light,
> true God from true God,
> begotten not made,
> of one being with the Father.

We sing this in the second verse of 'O Come, All Ye Faithful' but it may not be seen as helpful by today's questioners. Little wonder that some Christians seek happier terms than Son for today's world: Jesus as God's Agent, though this has detergent or MI5 connotations, or God's representative, though this seems like a holiday resort courier. Our man in Galilee, etc.! The quest for a new word picture is on, however.

For we have perhaps again lost sight of the

Doves in the Rat Race

picture language of words. Being in love, feeling despair, ecstasy, bereavement, God, cannot be captured in words, even the words of the poet. Some of the problems of the Sonship idea are problems caused by pressing words too far in an attempt to map out the Jesus–God link. The Fourth Gospel, with characteristic deep economy, notes that the Word, i.e. the living Word, Christ, 'was the same as God' (1.1).

Analogy must be used carefully. Jesus was like a Son. Here's another analogy. Press this too far and it becomes unhelpful. Picture a shop. We are the customers, so we can't go behind the Staff Only door into the back. Instead we see what the staff have created in their displays on the shelves and in the window. We see how they treat us. The business was set up a long time ago and no one now remembers the owner personally. He may be directing it from the back, behind the closed door. He may even have passed on into eternity. Yet the business is run according to his insights, his principles, his wishes, by people who understand him. Certainly it is as if he is in the shop, even though we can't see him. No doubt you've guessed that the manager is his son. He's very well qualified for the job, because he's been in the shop helping since he was a lad and the assistants agree that he is the closest to the boss. Although we don't know what is going on in the back, we know enough to trust that the shop will give us a fair deal. It is, after all, a father and son partnership.

So in the end, who is or was Jesus? How nice it

Christian Beliefs

would be if we could do a 'This is Your Life' on Jesus or as in the comedy quiz show say 'Will the real Jesus of Nazareth please stand up?' and the matter would be solved. We do not need to be endlessly pessimistic, however, for some things about Jesus can be recovered and accepted with reasonable probability. He does not need to remain a total enigma, though to a different age and culture there will always be aspects of Jesus which are hard to understand, even incomprehensible because of passing time and the incompleteness of the historical evidence that survives. It is important to recollect that evidence about Jesus survives in several forms:

in the New Testament – and we need to remind ourselves that the letters were written before the Gospels although the Gospels appear first in the order of books in the New Testament;

in Jewish sources of the first century AD, notably the historian Flavius Josephus;

in Roman sources about the growth of the Christian faith soon after Jesus, e.g. the letters of Pliny;

in archaeological evidence, e.g. in the catacombs of Rome or in Christian graffiti whose symbols provide clues to the beliefs of the first Christians;

in later Gospels which may contain some genuine material from Jesus' teaching or echoes of it, e.g. the Gospel of Thomas.

Of course the Four Gospels of the New Testament remain the main sources and we must not be offput by admitting with the sceptics that they are

Doves in the Rat Race

biased because Christians wrote them. All reporting is reporting from a point of view. 'Unbiased reporting' doesn't exist. For any reporter first selects what to write by excluding some material; the selection will reflect his interests and the interests of the readers. Comparing *The Times* and *The Sun* reports on the same issues will readily show that. Then the reporter will tell the story in a particular way or from a particular angle. This reflects his own experience or interests. What matters is that we, the readers, are aware of the bias so that if necessary we can compensate for it. The bias of the reporter does not, however, destroy the truth of the story. Whether Dunkirk was a disorganized, crushing defeat of the enemy (a possible Nazi view) or one of the finest moments of heroism and resistance in British history (a possible British view) is a matter of interpretation: but the facts of that evacuation in 1940 stand whichever interpretation is taken of them. This does not mean, however, when the Bible is the record in question, that we have to believe all of it or none of it. The nature of the Bible and its relevance for Christians is discussed more fully in the next section. Suffice to say here that a Christian is not expected to believe every single thing the Bible says about Jesus. They may choose to, but that isn't the same. Even the creeds, traditional statements of the faith, don't require Christians to do that.

So we can know things about Jesus: some of his teachings; some aspects of his personality; some of his activities, especially the closing days including

Christian Beliefs

the events leading up to the arrest, crucifixion and resurrection. We can also see the sense of his presence now among Christians. That is a sort of evidence, hard to evaluate, but still evidence. One strand runs through all this, the centrality of love. Those who become his disciples are called to live in a spirit of Christ-like love. Being a Christian might be as simple, and as difficult, as that.

3 · ABOUT THE BIBLE

One of the things that makes some outsiders hesitant about the Christian faith and at the same time makes some insiders feel guilty is the assumption that you are supposed to read the Bible every day – or night – and be improved by it. Honesty would compel many Christians to admit that they don't read it often, except for the members of the evangelical or 'Bible churches'. In these churches, and to some individual Christians in other denominations, the Bible is God's inspired Word, the rule for faith and life, a sort of guarantor of the tradition after Jesus himself ascended. They will attempt to run their churches and their personal lives by reference to it as a yardstick. This has not, sadly, prevented quarrels about its interpretation even among the Bible's staunchest supporters. For many other Christians, however, the Bible has no such central place. True, it is read aloud in worship, among the community for which it was written, and someone who was part of worship over some fifty Sundays per year would hear the most important parts read and perhaps expounded in the

Christian Beliefs

preaching. It seems to be read less nowadays in private devotion and a recent Archbishop of Canterbury referred to many modern Christians as biblically illiterate. Lent house study groups or special Bible reading notes are being used by some Christians to try to inject some discipline into their use of the Bible. There is still an unspoken feeling, in other Christian circles, that the Bible has gone out of fashion and somehow needs promoting.

In the 'Bible churches' no such promptings are needed. Literalists will see it as a natural and necessary staple diet and corner stone of the faith, if the metaphor isn't too crazily mixed! They will be impatient with attempts by other Christians to study the Bible critically, i.e. like other ancient texts. That may be seen as presumptuous, rather like interviewing God to see whether he is good enough for the job. The literalist has a simple rule of interpretation, which is that what the Bible says it means, at face value. It is to be obeyed rather than questioned, for through it God speaks. So the literalist is happy to accept that the Genesis creation account which talks of six days of creation means exactly that: six, not five or seven. The whole earth was really flooded, Jesus really walked on water, etc. How could God's word not be true? Science cannot therefore contradict it, so where science appears to conflict with the biblical account, for example the concept of evolution and a literal acceptance of Genesis 1 and 2, then it is science that must be mistaken. Rather surprisingly, perhaps, some scientists accept this view of the Bible,

Doves in the Rat Race

though those who do are more rarely from the discipline which appears to conflict with the Bible. Evolution is opposed by more physicists than biologists.

The literal view of the Bible is a very convenient view, if you can accept it, though even then it doesn't solve all problems, because the Bible appears to contradict itself in several places. For example, how did Judas die? The better known story in Matthew's Gospel suggests that he hanged himself (27.5). Luke, however, in his second book tells how a terrible accident happened to Judas (Acts 1.18). You can't have both! Exodus 21.24 insists on a system of justice based on the principle of an eye for an eye. Yet Jesus firmly rejects this as a basis for living (Matt. 5.38). And who killed Goliath? The little known Elhanan (II Sam. 21.19) or the more famous David (I Sam. 17)? What is certain is that there is no evidence to suggest that the two names are names for one and the same man. These are just a few examples of contradictions that pose no problems for most Bible readers, but because literalists are committed to defending the literal truth of the whole lot they pose massive problems for them. How do you explain them away?

But even if the contradictions are ignored, the Bible still has to be interpreted by any reader. Even literalists will interpret the Bible differently. For even where we might believe every word as literal truth we each interpret a passage in our own way, so some subjective element remains. So while it is

Christian Beliefs

of course quite possible to be a Christian and take a literalist view of the Bible, that does not solve all your problems of Bible study. It is also possible to be a Christian and approach the Bible quite differently.

One way of modifying the literalist view is the fundamentalist position. The fundamentalist believes the Bible to be fundamentally true, that is to say substantially or largely true, though not always literally true. The six days of Genesis could therefore be six epochs or periods of time. So if we are labelling approaches to the Bible this is still a conservative approach, but it is spared the need to fight to defend every dot and comma as inerrant. It is also spared the problem of which Greek text would be the inerrant base for the English translation, because it accepts that what has come down through the various texts is fundamentally reliable.

But there are more liberal or radical approaches to the Bible too. Fewer assumptions about the nature of the Bible are made here, except that it is like other books in having human origins, sources, writers, points of view, etc., which can be traced, as with other books, through intellectual or thoughtful study. That is not to say that God has not been working in the process, but the nature of God's operation in the process is seen as a matter for faith which does not prevent a full analysis of the book as a book.

Obviously this sort of approach is more subjective as it places on the reader the onus of working out, accepting, rejecting, piece by piece. Not

Doves in the Rat Race

surprisingly the findings of liberal scholars have been more varied than those of conservative scholars. Despite these difficulties it is, however, for many Christians the only honest way to study the Bible now and it is not subject to the house of cards effect; if you reject one section or passage you don't have to reject the whole lot. It doesn't crumble, whereas once a literalist rejects a passage they've lost the lot.

'Radical' Christians are perhaps more sceptical still than mere liberals. The word itself means getting back to the roots and radicals have been willing to surrender much more of the literal and historical truth of the text to get at its centre, which they perceive to be religious or personal truth, in which the details of the accounts, or even the accounts themselves, play very much second place. Small wonder that liberal and literalist Christians do battle from time to time and the pronoucements of radical bishops are still of interest to the media.

So it is vital that Christians and outsiders begin to see that it is not a case of 'Do you believe the Bible?' with its assumption that you believe the whole of it or none of it. The whole matter is infinitely more subtle than that. That can be liberating news to honest outsiders who thought they were being called upon to believe all sorts of things they really doubted before they could become Christians. For me as a teenager it was a good news that you could believe and question, even reject, some of the accounts.

In order to appreciate the different approaches to

Christian Beliefs

the Bible we can examine a particular passage. Let's take Mark 6.45–52, the story of Jesus walking on the water. I wonder how many readers were told this story, with no attempt to interpret it, at primary school. I would view this as a prime example of a piece of unsuitable material for small children. What we are looking at here, however, is how differently it can be interpreted by adult readers.

> At once Jesus made his disciples get into the boat and go ahead of him to Bethsaida, on the other side of the lake, while he sent the crowd away. After saying goodbye to the people he went away to a hill to pray. When evening came, the boat was in the middle of the lake, while Jesus was alone on land. He saw that his disciples were straining at the oars, because they were rowing against the wind, so some time between three and six o'clock in the morning he came to them, walking on the water. 'It's a ghost!' they thought, and screamed. They were all terrified when they saw him. Jesus spoke to them at once. 'Courage!' he said. 'It is I. Don't be afraid!' Then he got into the boat with them, and the wind died down. The disciples were completely amazed, because they had not understood the real meaning of the feeding of the five thousand; their minds could not grasp it.

The literalist and fundamentalist would argue that this narrative is historically true, for reasons like these:

Doves in the Rat Race

the Bible says it happened, so it did;

since Jesus was the Son of God he would have had power, God's power, to do this. It would have been simple to him;

Christian tradition has long held that Mark got his information from the disciple Peter, who would have been present at this event. So other than prejudice against miracles, you have to have better reasons for thinking it didn't happen.

A liberal or radical might interpret this passage differently, arguing points like these:

people don't walk on water. Such behaviour is not scientifically possible for humans. If Jesus was human, he too could not have behaved in such a way any more than he could have flown;

nevertheless some event must have occurred to produce this story, which is here used like a parable ... But it would be a mistake to concentrate on what happened rather than the meaning and beliefs behind it;

the sea, to Jews of Jesus' day, represented chaos and the forces of evil. It was the 'raging ocean' of Gen. 1.2 that had to be tamed before creation could really begin. See also Ps. 89.9. By presenting Jesus as a sea-tamer, Mark is showing the power of Jesus to equal the power of God in the Genesis account. In other words the real meaning of the story is to shed light on who, according to Mark, Jesus is, rather than on what he did.

For many people, however, the authority of the Bible and how you should study it is not the problem. The problem is more basic. How do you

Christian Beliefs

understand a 2000-year old text and isn't it boring or irrelevant? There are no slick answers to these questions, especially in a generation where it is widely believed that the Bible is boring, mainly by people who haven't read it, or who read part of it when they were too young and were put off.

But commentaries, written to explain individual books and passages as you read them, abound. They will obligingly reflect your own approach to the Bible, i.e. some are conservative and some are liberal and you read the back cover and the introduction or look up some passage such as John 2 (the wedding at Cana, where it is said that Jesus turned water into wine) and see what the commentator does to it in interpreting it. These commentary books can make the Bible understandable for today's society. So can group study. In a Christian Bible study group you can get insights into a passage, sometimes devotional, sometimes academic, that you would not have got alone. You also have the stimulus and discipline of the weekly passage to prepare before the meeting and the chance to think about it after.

For however unfashionable it may become, even among some Christians, to study the Bible, it remains to liberal and conservative alike the key document of the faith. It is a storehouse of Jewish and Christian experience, even though culture and society have moved on. Human nature doesn't seem to have moved much, which means that the insights of the Bible into human nature are ever fresh. One example of this is the Adam and Eve

Doves in the Rat Race

story. Whether or not it is history it is true to what human nature is like – we feel cut off from God, we instinctively do what we are told not to do, we blame others when we are caught out etc. So the Bible provides not rules but insights. There is no section on what Christians should believe about nuclear war, but there's lots about attitudes to our enemies and to evil, that require patient, detailed study and then the attempt to apply it to today's world.

We tend to take for granted that the Bible is the chief, though not the only source, for information about the life of Jesus. Whether we read it as conservative or liberal, as believer or agnostic, accepting all or some of it, Jesus comes over as a human being of enormous courage, depth and love and, by any standard, a spiritual giant. At least! So for the Christian the Bible is a sort of witness to Jesus, not a history book or a biography in any modern sense, for the ancients didn't write history like we do: they didn't indicate the sources they used; they wrote speeches for some of the characters they describe; and they didn't pretend as we so often do to be unbiased. They knew that history isn't fact. It's interpretation, from a point of view. The New Testament provides us with a witness to Jesus. This is not always (or some would say, even), eyewitness, but then eyewitnesses are sometimes too close to see the details and remember them. They bring a power of feeling to their description, however, which more than compensates for blurring of detail.

Christian Beliefs

There are of course twentieth-century Christian writings to supplement the Bible, and the pick of previous centuries too: *The Imitation of Christ*, *The Little Flowers of St Francis*, Wesley's *Journals*, William Booth's *In Darkest England and the Way Out* etc., but the writings of our time attempt to apply biblical insights to today's world. These are not commentaries on passages but insights into Christian living with a biblical perspective. They are no substitute for the Bible but they may help Christians over dry patches in their study of the Bible and they may complement the Bible by applying biblical insights into modern situations. In this they may be helped by Christian newspapers and magazines in which the latest events within the denominational or wider Christian community along with Christian insights into current affairs can be brought to the reader's attention.

The different versions and translations of the Bible may also help us to see the meaning of a passage because the translations vary and offer new slants on the meaning of the text. It is always useful to have at least two modern translations so that perplexing passages can be compared. The Good News Bible (Bible Society/Collins) makes a fine start. There are also interesting collections like *Best Bible Bits* (ed. Janet Green, CIO Publishing 1984) in which famous people were asked to choose their favourite Bible passage and say why. Ronnie Barker, Ernie Wise, Arthur Scargill, Mrs Thatcher and Prince Charles are numbered among the book's subjects and their choice of passage is quoted. Food for thought there!

Doves in the Rat Race

At the end of all this, however, the best way to see the Bible is as a book of inspiration for Christians now, not a page by page manual of doctrine or devotion. They should read some of it! Those interested in reading the Bible but perhaps unsure where to begin should read the Gospel of Mark and I Corinthians, with appropriate commentaries. These two documents are short enough to be read at one or two sittings each and as we have seen do not have to be read on a take it or leave it basis. They provide a vivid insight into the early Christian community and into the writer's view of Jesus. Read without comparison with other Gospels or letters, they can be quite stunning. For those unused to reading the Bible or used only to reading or hearing extracts they provide an excellent starting point. It was S. T. Coleridge, better remembered now for his poetry, who first suggested that we should read the Bible like any other book. We should then, he was convinced, find it to be unlike any other book and whatever 'finds me' in its pages bears witness, he said, to the holy spirit.

4 · ABOUT THE NEXT WORLD

At present within Christianity there seems to be almost a conspiracy of silence on this matter, except among some evangelical or fundamentalist circles. These groups are quite sure, because of statements in the Bible, where Paul actually talks more about it in his letters than Jesus does in the Gospels, that there will be a life beyond death and that it is guaranteed to faithful Christians. Interestingly, when you read what Paul says about it he changes his own view on the details between what he says in I Thessalonians (4.13–18), which is generally reckoned to be one of the earliest letters, dating from about AD 40 and what he says ten years later in I Corinthians 15. These writings, the resurrection of Jesus himself and the visionary promises of Revelation 21 and 22 form the basis of comforting passages within the Christian funeral service.

But few sermons are preached on this topic in Sunday services, especially among 'liberal' Christians. Why? There may be a natural lack of confidence about speaking of a state of being which

Doves in the Rat Race

words from our present state can barely describe. Paul realized this, in writing that: 'What is made of flesh and blood cannot share in God's Kingdom and what is mortal cannot possess immortality' (I Cor. 15.50). It is also true that Christianity is currently very much involved in living in this world, trying to combat world hunger, social injustice and emphasizing the 'here and now' rather than being accused of offering dubiously provable rewards for later. We may be in reaction against the Victorians, for whom death was a more present daily experience than it is for us, and for whom even children were inducted into firm beliefs about the pleasures of heaven and the torments of hell. Clearly the fear of hell was used to frighten people into a code of moral behaviour that it was felt their sinful natures would otherwise kick against. We would not want to threaten our tiny tots with hell fire.

Some other faiths tackle death with more openness and resolve. The prophet Muhammad taught Muslims to visit the cemetery often to reflect on life, death and the life to come. This is done in a non-morbid way. On the other hand we Westerners have sanitized death so that it is rarely seen and rarely acknowledged. Patients are 'lost', relatives 'pass away' and we rush into the security of our unquestioning routines to avoid further thoughts. This dodges the issue.

Christians are entitled to ask, even where they are not content to accept the evidence of the Bible alone, whether death is the end. 'Scientific' evidence

Christian Beliefs

is unclear, though videos and books exist in which people who have 'died' discuss their post-death experience before they were revived on the mortuary slab. There is a pattern to such experiences which may include a sensation of looking down at one's body, a feeling of progression through a tunnel, the sensation of light at the end of it, and sometimes of faces of people one knew coming to meet one, along with a feeling of great liberation and often a resistance to going back to one's body. What is interesting about these experiences is that they cut across social class, intelligence, culture, religion and even include atheists. This suggests a genuineness. But there the discussion ends, for one can be genuinely mistaken and, fascinating as these experiences are to study, they are not proof of any after life, for all the subjects returned to this life relatively quickly. No one went for three days!

That reference isn't meant facetiously. The resurrection of Jesus is still very much what the Greeks called ephapax and we call a one-off. We need to approach it with caution, first checking our own prejudice. In other words if we are convinced people never have, never could, never will survive death, not even one person, we shall approach the resurrection programmed to find some alternative explanation. If we are convinced before we start that every word of the Bible is literally true we shall accept the resurrection accounts without question and we shall be unsympathetic to Christians who are interested, intellectually or out of curiosity, in examining the detail and questioning the accounts.

Doves in the Rat Race

Once we've come to terms with our own prejudice we could look carefully at the accounts, including the forgotten one by Paul in I Corinthians 15, which pre-dates the Gospels by at least fifteen years. While Luke grounds himself firmly in his concern for history (1.1–4) he is keen to assert that Jesus was not a ghost since he ate boiled fish (24.37–43). Luke is equally concerned to assert that Jesus appears now where Christians meet together and share his bread (24.13–35). Similarly in the Gospel of John, Jesus appears in rooms with locked doors, where his followers are present, and doubting Thomas can examine his wounds (20.19–29). I think it is significant that he was not seen by complete unbelievers, and even some believers doubted (Matt. 28.17).

What significance is it that it seems the sceptics didn't see him? The sceptics' answer is that the believers made up or imagined his appearances. Both are possible. The first is unlikely. Unlikely because they had no motive. They didn't become famous, in their life times; they didn't make money out of it; preaching the resurrection earned scorn and persecution. Whether they imagined it depends on our own prejudices about the sort of people the disciples were. If you think they were simpletons, then maybe they would have imagined it, though history doesn't exactly abound with mass hallucinations. If they were uneducated but nevertheless hard-headed, common-sense folk, then delusions are less likely. The anti-resurrection case has its own questions to answer: did Jesus revive, in the

Christian Beliefs

pitch dark stone-sealed tomb, and 'con' people? And if so, when did he die and why wasn't that used to discredit Christianity? If the disciples stole his body, another improbable possibility, why did they do it and what happened to it? Yet none of this constitutes proof of the resurrection. We have to make a personal judgment based on all the many aspects mentioned. My answer to why only believers saw him is simply this: it wasn't because they were expecting to see him, believing him to be dead, but they were half-prepared to recognize him because of the references he had made to it, enigmatically, during his ministry (Mark 8.31–33; 9.30–32; 10.32–34 etc.). The eyes of the others were closed by his death. If you are not expecting to see even your husband or wife in a particular place you may walk, unnoticing, past them in the street. Many married couples can tell this story. Still less will you be looking for someone whom you knew to be dead. Moreover, the accounts of the resurrection appearances are tantalizing: Jesus was the same, recognizable to his friends, talking, walking, eating, but yet different, mysteriously arriving and disappearing.

There are no provable facts except one: the faith that the first Christians had in the resurrection changed their lives, brought into being the church and gave them the hope that while Jesus was present now in this world in the breaking of bread, in the needs of our neighbour (Matt. 25.31–46) and in the Christian community where even two or three meet in his name, they would share in his

Doves in the Rat Race

defeat of death and in the fullness of God's Kingdom.

Jesus himself believed in an after-life, one of the few things he agreed with his enemies the Pharisees about (Mark 12.18–27). He referred to it as a non-earthly type of existence (Mark 12.25) where earthly institutions such as marriage and presumably jobs, eating etc. have given place to an existence 'like the angels' which, alas, he didn't elaborate. Perhaps to some people such an existence seems boring: 'I've been in heaven now for 5,567,892 years, six months, four days, three hours and twenty-seven minutes and I'm fed up with singing hymns!' Such a view forgets that time is a human invention. Even we rise above it when we're happy and then declare it's 'flown'. Perhaps in the after-life it will have flown altogether.

Possibly the best philosophical argument for an after-life is based on the nature of God, as understood by Christians. If God is love, his love is undefeatable. So after Auschwitz, Belsen and the others which we human beings built, and the famines we might cure if we stopped buying bombs, there has to be something better. Death cannot kill undying love. William Penn put it in these words in 1693 and they are a reminder that poetry can be used to help us cross the boundary:

> The truest end of life, is to know the Life that never ends.
> He that makes this his Care, will find it his crown at last.

Christian Beliefs

And he that lives to live ever, never fears dying:
nor can the means be terrible to him
that heartily believes the end.

For though Death be a Dark passage, it leads to Immortality,
And that's Recompence enough for Suffering of it.
And yet Faith lights us even through the Grave,
being Evidence of Things not seen.

And this is the Comfort of the Good,
that the Grave cannot hold them,
and that they live as soon as they die.
For Death is no more
than a turning over of us from time to eternity.
Death, then, being the way and condition of Life,
we cannot love to live,
if we cannot bear to die.

They that love beyond the World, cannot be separated by it.
Death cannot kill what never dies.
Nor can Spirits ever be divided
that love and live in the same Divine Principle,
the Root and Record of their Friendship.
If Absence be not Death, neither is theirs.

Death is but Crossing the World, as Friends do the Seas;
they live in one another still.

Doves in the Rat Race

For they must needs be present,
that love and live in that which is Omnipresent.
In this Divine Glass, they see Face to Face;
and their Converse is Free, as well as Pure.

PART THREE
Christian Behaviour

1 · THE MORAL IMAGE: SEX AND LOVING

At the moment moral values appear to be in a state of flux. With the rise of the permissive society in the 1960s it seemed that the churches were often trying to put the brakes on, ineffectually, and in a rather spoilsport way. They appeared to be telling people that they couldn't do what they really wanted to do, and they must bridle what was felt to be 'natural'. We may note in passing that natural is a strange word, because violence is natural but we may properly strive to eliminate it in society. The churches appeared in this guise because they didn't have the cash or advertising backing or the public relations know-how to see that, deliberately or otherwise, they were being pushed into a corner so that the brakes could really come off and another more shadowy group of people with their own axes to grind could grind them for a while. Once this had begun to happen, of course, the more stridently the churches protested, the more they appeared to be conforming to this Thou-shalt-not

Doves in the Rat Race

puritan image. It has always been the case that whatever preachers urge on such potent issues as sexual behaviour, in which we are all involved because we are all sexual beings, their hearers will continue to rationalize their urges and do what they choose!

The so-called Christian ethic was punctured, however, because without the beliefs to undergird it, the reasons for behaving in particular ways disappeared. 'Why shouldn't we?' began to look as if it was an unanswerable question. It was easy to parody the church's position as an over-concern with genital behaviour rather than a concern for respect and for loving, which people would have to translate into practice for themselves. So without realizing that the growing power of the pop sub-cults and the fashion scene were manipulating them every bit as much as the churches had failed to do, people began to absorb another, unwritten set of values — that life was about enjoyment, having a good time, satisfying yourself. Of course all this arose at a time when teenagers in particular were beginning to have more to spend than they'd ever had before, and more than their parents, whose mortgage commitments, etc. swallowed their incomes.

It was assumed that life owed us certain things: a rising standard of living, a job and personal enjoyment. This enjoyment was understood as essentially an enjoyment of the physical and material; it was about obtaining more clothes, records and possessions; it was about obtaining more 'good'

Christian Behaviour

experiences for oneself, and so the drug sub-cults pushed to legalize the allegedly less harmful ones. Part of these assumptions that life owed you pleasures and thrills was the public change in attitudes towards sexuality. There are difficulties about making accurate pronouncements about private sexual behaviour, then, now or before, because even where surveys are carried out there is no guarantee that people will speak honestly on such matters. They may feel obliged to claim experience they haven't had or to conform to what they see as the social norm. Some say: 'Everybody does it.' There is no way in which that statement can be proved or disproved, but it is interesting that it is believed, or used in such a way as to affect the behaviour of others. In other words it may help me to bed you if I can use this sort of pressure, because you are then cornered like the churches into giving an against-the-stream and prudish refusal. This new emphasis in personal morality was coupled with a proviso: you can do whatever you like, as long as you don't hurt anyone else. But hurt was construed in a limited and physical sense. In other words you couldn't rape someone because you fancied them. That was still, fortunately, taboo. But you could live with them if they consented and leave them whenever you felt you needed a change because, it was said, that was the whole point; you weren't involved in complex legal ties to inhibit your enjoyment. What parting did to your partner's emotions was never part of the equation in this sexual equivalent of convenience food. When you

Doves in the Rat Race

had tossed the package away it ceased to be your concern. In these heady days of pure enjoyment the casualties of this sort of living were not, as some asserted, the VD statistics – it can hardly be seen as Christian to peddle fear of disease as a basis for morality – it was the broken hearts. Alas, the churches seemed to emphasize the disease risk as the prominent problem. What was missing in Christian witness, at a popular level, was a critique of the basic assumption here: that each of us is an independent, morally autonomous being, able to live for ourselves as long as we acted legally. Whether the broken-hearted in these abandoned relationships were damaged permanently and entered subsequent relationships more casually cannot be assessed as there is no hard evidence one way or the other.

Fashion is now changing. The mid and late eighties ushered in a period of reaction. The rise of AIDS reinforced all sorts of guilts that permissiveness was not a right way to proceed and it was a sign of the new times that the tolerance shown to homosexuals decreased. How far this reaction will go remains to be seen. What is clear is that Christians need to be careful, whatever the current fashion is, not to be carried along by the spirit of the age. The cure of AIDS and VD could change morality just as quickly again, one day, as the pill is said to have done in the past. It is vital to see, however, that fashionable social morality, the spirit of the age, and a loving, Christian basis for behaviour are not always the same. This is difficult

Christian Behaviour

because most of us absorb the spirit of the age in which we grow up without question, just as once the so-called Christian ethic was assumed, then the permissive ethic and now a time of uncertainty.

Christians should not be driven by these strong tides. There are other strong tides within each of us too, the tides of our own feelings and emotions. It is always easy to rationalize our own feelings and do what we want to do or ban what we want to ban, all in the name of some glorious principle. Glorious twaddle! We need to watch ourselves most carefully when our feelings are part of any major decision; no need to suppress them, but we do need to be aware where they are taking us. In a physical or sexual relationship we are especially vulnerable to cloaking our feelings in some other guise to justify a course of action.

At the same time Christians have passed beyond the view that you can legislate physical feelings and relationships into a set of rules as to what you can do, when, where you can put your hands and how soon in a relationship, etc. A more suitable approach now might be applied to any relationship, whether 'platonic', sexual, child–parent or whatever and it is to ask the searching questions:

Is the relationship a fulfilling and creative one for both/all the parties involved? Am I allowing my desires/needs to over-ride those of my partner/ the others in the relationship? Do they need me more than I need them, and if so am I sensitive to this in my treatment of them? Is their assessment of the relationship the same as mine?

Doves in the Rat Race

Behind these questions lies a sure Christian principle, if we are searching for one, that no relationship can be a right one which manipulates other people or uses them as a means to my gratification. Whether the other person is a prostitute, a husband, a child or a parent or 'just a good friend', and whether the relationship is friendship or friendship of a particular kind, the principle applies just as keenly.

For women and men such a principle would usually involve marriage as the basis for a deep and lasting relationship, though one could think of exceptions to this. Homosexuality has become hotly debated among Christians again and attitudes vary from total acceptance, through acceptance of the condition but not the practice, to total rejection as an illness requiring treatment or a sin requiring repentance. When we discuss this we have to be careful that our own strong emotions, towards homosexuality or against it, don't colour the discussion too much. Perhaps it has in common with divorce that while many Christians regret it, they have come to accept it as a fact of life. Better to accept it as a fact of life and get on with developing in ourselves and in our own relationships qualities of love and of forgiveness and of listening. Christians always become their least convincing when they reject Jesus' strong advice and start sitting in judgment on individuals and groups. This is the time to re-read Matt. 7.1–5.

Certainly the churches could contribute more to reducing the stress that Western marriage appears

Christian Behaviour

to be under. It may be that there are initiatives in marriage guidance and in training counsellors in which Christians could help. Perhaps the wedding service itself should emphasize our Christian experience that, like all relationships, marriage has to be worked at to be kept going. As part of the Jewish wedding ceremony the bridegroom breaks a wine glass under his foot, suitably wrapped in a handkerchief – the glass, not the foot! While the origins of this custom are lost, it is widely held that it represents a reminder of the bitter times marriage will bring, as well as the happiness. Despite threats about for richer for poorer, for better for worse, sickness and health, the Christian ceremony might benefit from some similar ingredient. You can't just assume marriage will last, any more than you can assume that the friendship with the person to whom you only send an annual Christmas card and letter but never see, will endure. Sometimes marriages fall into the trap of acting as if you don't need to run for the bus when you've caught it. That road leads to the terminus!

Another opportunity the churches have, through the large numbers who still use them for weddings, is to emphasize that Western marriage has perhaps become too sexually orientated with self-gratification as the major part. It would be injudicious to point this out at the altar! Nevertheless the wedding preparation class needs to explore perceptions of marriage. My experience as a teacher of adolescents is that their dominant perception of marriage is as a passport to a sexual bonanza with a partner you

Doves in the Rat Race

really 'fancy'. As Christians we need the honesty to point out that it is hard to see a successful marriage without a successful and developing sexual relationship, but it is equally hard to see a successful marriage based only on the sexual, for in that case when the fires cool or you reach the age of thirty or forty you begin to look for sexual satisfaction elsewhere. In such cases the seeds of the divorce have been sown before the wedding day.

There is another need, however, to which Christians have to respond, and that is the vulnerability of human beings. Indeed, some are more vulnerable than others! Not sitting in judgment on the moral behaviour of others is fine, scriptural, Christian, but are we providing a positive spiritual and moral basis for relationships in our families and churches? Avoiding negative condemnation is not enough. Positive advice is needed. If we trumpet the moral autonomy of mankind too strongly, swept along by the fashion of our time, we become permissive again. A humbler view would be more Christ-like. This could start with our need for acceptance. We all need friends; we all need affection; we are all easily hurt, emotionally, if our weak points are touched. In fact we are all morally vulnerable. That is the real truth and a painful one for some to acknowledge. What better way to run away from vulnerability than by trumpeting the opposite – autonomy – as the basis of the human condition?

Sexuality is only one aspect of how we relate to others and should not be seen too much in

Christian Behaviour

isolation. How should we bring up our children? What sort of rewards and punishments are 'Christian'? What should we tell them about say, homosexuals? Does our embarrassment at our children discovering that their parents have sexual feelings cripple our attempts to help them with and through relationships? What exactly do we owe our elderly parents? These are all hot moral issues that are easy to shelve until they hit us. The upshot of all this is that, far from being ended by either the permissive society or the new reaction, the moral debate has hardly begun. Christians have a vital contribution to make to it which must be more than an uncritical acceptance of the fashionable spirit of the age. It will be hard to find and then make public what this contribution might be, because for lots of churches and lots of individual Christians the process of disentangling their new view of right and wrong from the fashions of the time in which they have been brought up will be long and perhaps painful. If Christianity is to endure as other than a prop for the moral values of a supposedly Christian West, it will have to be done.

2 · AT HOME

It is perhaps strange that the Christian faith seems to have lost what family base it may have had. By contrast in Judaism all the vitally important aspects, or at least many of them, are centred in the home and family rather than in the synagogue alone: circumcision, the weekly sabbath meal, the dietary observance, the festivals and especially passover – all are home based. This is the case in other faiths where family worship may occur regularly: the Hindu home will have its small shrine. The Sikh family will put on their religiously significant clothing. The Muslim mother may teach her small children the first steps in the way of the Qur'an. In the Christian family ... what?

There may be just a residue. Grace may be said before meals regularly or occasionally. Perhaps the idea of the church as a Christian family has replaced the idea of the blood-related family as a Christian family. That's fine, if the reality of the local church fits the theory. It is only Mormon Christianity which sets aside a family day in which worship together and recreation as a shared activity are the

Christian Behaviour

components. Of course there are exceptions. Some families still read the Bible together. Some pray. But as a generalization it is true that most Christians do not locate their devotional life or its centre within the home.

This is not entirely regrettable. It may spare the embarrassment of teenage questioning or open rebellion at rituals the youngster is no longer taking for granted. It may avoid the awkwardness of compelling or pressuring the visitor or friend of the children into joining in. It may protect the parents from a religious responsibility they feel inadequate to carry alone. Certainly lack of religious observance in the home removes the vital questions as to the age at which you allow the children to opt out. But something is missing. Perhaps in practice there is a conspiracy of silence and the parents don't show their children their religious behaviour or their own observance. That would deprive children both of Christian example and of an aspect of their parents' life that need not be private. Perhaps it points to another issue – that many couples have no spiritual life together. Even so, leaving most of it to church need not be bad, as long as the church in question behaves like a Christian family and as long as the family from home attend it regularly enough for it to be a natural part of their family life. If attendance comes once in a blue moon the children will not see its relevance to the lives of their parents and hence to their own.

So what are the duties of the Christian parent? Many make promises at child baptism that they fail

Doves in the Rat Race

to deliver later, and parents and godparents must ponder whether this is not hypocritical and undermining of real religion. Similarly it would be humbug to pray over a child or to pray at home the prayers we think the child ought to hear, that would be 'good' for her or him, if they are not our own natural prayers. Buying a prayer book or Bible for children, pressing it into their hands and leaving them to it is the biggest dodge of all, for bookish religion has never been real religion, as the prophets of the Jewish religion reminded their hearers centuries before Christ. The child ought to be as much a part of the adult's spiritual life as their maturity will allow; adults need sensitively to share with their children what they do by way of Bible reading, reflection, prayer etc., without imposing it as a drudgery. It must not be seen by the child as so precious that the child feels unable to ask questions or comment about it.

Relating to the age of the child matters. Infant prayers and phrases will offend juniors. The child's own experiences need to be part of the family effort to share spirituality. It is often at bedtime where in the quiet talk, so much can come out, even with adolescents. They, too, need to talk out the day and their joys and sorrows just as much as the small child, but they want to choose the time to do it. It is a wise parent who doesn't try to force the pace. More often the parents become tongue-tied in discussing their beliefs and especially their doubts with their children and feel, unreasonably, that they should defend the Christian view, even where

Christian Behaviour

there may be several possible Christian views or even where they don't share it. It is better to be honest. More often they may just feel inadequate to deal with the child's questions. This is where church house discussion groups can be so important in the continuing Christian education of the adults. For it is another misconception by many that just as your education ends on the day you leave school, your Christian education ends on the day you are received into church membership or confirmed.

Just as children will sense the embarrassment of their parents in discussing sexual issues they will also sense it on religious issues and the whole area can become a taboo subject. Yet certain times demand that religious questions and issues are raised in the home. Christmas is one of these times. It would be a failure on the part of parents sympathetic to Christianity not to make more of Christmas than the Gimme, gimme, gimme demands of small children, and to make more of Easter than just chocolate covered children as they become engulfed in extravagance! Baby Jesus should always remain central rather than Father Christmas and Jesus' new life should take precedence over the reproductive capacity of rabbits in the spring.

Another family occasion which demands some sharing of Christian doubts and conviction is when a death occurs. Although death is less of a taboo subject than perhaps even ten years ago it is still spoken of with reluctance by many adults. They

Doves in the Rat Race

don't want to upset people – perhaps themselves – and therefore repress the way in which the death of someone close to us calls into question our own routines and attitudes to life and makes us face the issue: where have they gone? Do they have a continuing life? Should we, if we are Christians, rejoice for them as well as grieve for them? How do we envisage their continuing existence, if we believe in it? These questions are better discussed than repressed and we may learn from our children. What no parent should ever do is to use Christianity to shut children up, as in this sort of debate:

Mummy, where's Grandma gone?

She, er, she's gone away.

Why's she gone away? I thought she liked us.

She did, dear, but, er, Jesus took her.

Why?

He wanted her to be with him in the sky.

Well, I wanted her here with us. Don't you?

Well, er, yes dear.

Will the Russians be able to see her from their orbitting space station?

Now, why don't you run along and play with your sister?

Almost every mistake in the Christian book is contained in incidents like this: using beliefs we don't hold to shut children up; presenting Jesus as a rather threatening figure who spirits away people we love; the implication that we might see Grandma from the aeroplane window when we next fly to the Costa del Sol; then trying to put the lid on a runaway discussion, leaving all the basic questions unanswered.

Christian Behaviour

In a different vein, it may be that worship in the home as opposed to discussion about religion seems to many families artificial or forced and they feel that worship within the wider Christian community is less inhibiting. This doesn't reduce the need for families that are Christian or sympathetic to the Christian faith to talk openly about it to one another and to talk through and reflect on Christian festivals and on crises such as bereavement. It doesn't reduce the need to provide for adults and children suitable Christian literature and, if appropriate, videos for reading, viewing and reflection. We readily seem to admit all sorts of influences via TV, newspapers, pop magazines and comics into our homes. These influences make all sorts of moral assumptions that we would not necessarily share. At the same time strict censorship is self-defeating: it may produce a strong interest in children in just what is being censored and a determination to read or see some of it – when they next go to a friend's house. Nor will censorship of a rigid sort help them to cope in the long run with the 'real' world. So while I am not of course suggesting that a Christian home would contain blue movies, horror videos etc. it is possible to go 'over the top' in filtering what is left around for children. If it's suitable for Christian adults, we have to be clear why it isn't suitable for Christian children. What is needed more than censorship alongside this varied material is a Christian perspective too. Part of this provision of books should include commentaries and background books on

Doves in the Rat Race

the Bible, for we shouldn't expect to pick up and understand any other text that was several thousands of years old without help. This one is no different in that respect and we shall be helping the whole family including ourselves if attractive and readable books to help us to understand the Bible are available.

The question of how far Christianity impinges on or should impinge on family life now is a big one. I have devoted a book to this issue, *Onward Christian Parents* (Church House Publishing 1986). Those interested can pursue the matter there.

3 · IN THE WORLD

Although our family and friends are undoubtedly nearer to the centre of our selves than our colleagues at work or school, it is in the wider social arenas of work, school, the dole queue and the contacts that arise from our hobbies that the people we meet look at our faith, and look at it hard. This is a test of our sincerity. Their tendency to criticize may be increased by the desire to prove to themselves that they are right not to take religion seriously. We ourselves may put them off from sampling faith further, either by being too otherworldly or by being too much one of the boys. In this latter case if we play along in language and behaviour, anxious to prove our normality, our contacts may accept us as one of them, no different at all. They will then view our profession on Sunday as hypocritical or at best a Sunday morning option for those who can wash the car at some other time. 'She goes to church and she's no better than we are.' Outsiders expect that beliefs should be reflected in behaviour. To some extent this feeling is understandable. In another sense it is like

Doves in the Rat Race

the double-think that expects vicars to be holier than us. Very unreasonable! Is it fair to expect Christians to be morally perfect beings? Would such beings be nice to know? Yet however hard I fought against this view rationally, my own view of one denomination was for a long time prejudiced by the fact that the only member I'd ever really known was awkward, prickly and hard to relate to. I was a nipper of thirty at the time! So much for maturity. I feel even more uncomfortable now in the knowledge that people may be reacting to me in the same way as I did on those occasions in the past.

People outside Christianity don't just look at the sort of people we are. They watch our reaction to certain stimuli – soft porn, bad language, the dirty joke, drunkenness – the socially risqué or perhaps acceptable harvest of our time. We may wonder whether there is any honest Christian reaction which avoids prudishness at one extreme and total acquiescence at the other. We may need to be honest first with ourselves. If these things are wrong and harmful, why are they objectionable? When we are sure where we stand on these issues we need the courage to stand by our view without sitting in judgment on those with differing views.

This sort of attitude, a sort of pragmatic Christianity, has to be the basis for the 'in the world but not of the world' of the rapidly changing world of today. Otherwise Christianity deteriorates into a rigid set of moral rules of increasing outmodedness. For while we may have to say No to certain stimuli or situations we need to remember that it

Christian Behaviour

would be a poor sort of faith that to outsiders looked like a set of Thou-shalt-nots, however defensible each one was individually. Setting a good example, communicating the positive, life-affirming things in Christianity, go a lot further than simply condemning 'the world'. Having said that, it may be valuable to look at some of these areas where a Christian set of values may appear to be in collision with the prevailing values of our times. To become caught up in the spirit of the age, whether it be permissiveness or puritanism, is always a snare for the Christian.

Certainly the spirit of our age seems to find alcohol abuse acceptable. The drunk has become a cartoon figure and the over-boisterousness of the merry person at a party finds ready excusers. The inconsiderateness and the vomit and the risk-taking with cars receive less attention, except in police and government attempts to bridle excesses. Parents are not always alive to the alcohol abuse at some teenage parties. Of course as Christians we need to be charitable. Anybody could get drunk once if they don't know what their level is with this potent and depressive drug, but to go out deliberately to get drunk as a perverse form of status seeking or entertainment seems an abuse of the body and an offence to our fellow human beings who have to sort us out. At its extreme it means an irresponsible use of hospital casualty department time and tragic, unnecessary deaths, usually of the innocent.

In the light of all this it is easy to see why some Christians, notably the Salvation Army, but many

Doves in the Rat Race

groups or individuals within other denominations, feel compelled to take a totally abstinent position as a matter of example and principle. Is this a parallel to the argument that would ban the sale of fireworks because they are misused and people are maimed and injured as a result? It runs deeper, because of course fireworks are not addictive and do not, in an abuse situation, ruin family life, bring on bankruptcy, wreck jobs etc.

But I brew home-made wine. So do some vicars. There is another Christian view that uses some alcoholic drinks, especially as an accompaniment to meals because the body and flavour are not found in other drinks. Such a view still finds drunkenness, drinking and driving etc., unacceptable, but the emphasis is on the old-fashioned word moderation and it is possibly better to teach one's children to drink in a controlled way like this within the family than to leave them to adolescent dares and under-age drinking. The recent rise of non-alcoholic wines and beers marketed on a large scale may give no excuse at all for not being TT if the body and flavour of the drink can be maintained without the alcohol. As these drinks are developed and their range and flavour extended, an unexpected consequence might be to make the Christian case for total abstinence stronger than ever before.

In contrast to the problem of over-drinking, the dirty joke is based on a strange form of blackmail. It is based on adolescent sexual awareness. You know that I know that you know it's the human sexual act and the personal parts of the body we are

Christian Behaviour

sniggering at. If you don't laugh it proves one of two things – either you are a Victorian prude or you don't get the point, in which case you are not sexually aware. So the pressure is on to laugh. We could produce a halt by asking in a loud voice exactly why the teller thought it was funny, but this could be a sure way of losing friends! What a pity that as Christians we so often fail to emphasize that sex is a gift from God and that loving sexual activities within a loving partnership, usually though not always on the basis of marriage, can be fun, healthy, refreshing for their own sake, not merely as a means to produce children. We're so apologetic about it!

It is grudgingly acknowledged to be enjoyable and even that is reckoned as a sign of weakness. How much healthier to enjoy sexual pleasures in a context of Christian love rather than giggle at the writing on the toilet wall transposed into a joke.

Bad language is another stimulus to which our response is watched. 'He's a vicar but he swears like a trooper,' is an insult or a compliment depending on who is saying it. Bad language is clearly socially unacceptable in certain situations. Pub, factory, school, office and home have their own but differing standards of acceptability. It is also clear that some words are less socially acceptable than others, even though we all know what the unacceptable ones are. Such little words seem to cause such great offence. These are social conventions of our time and will change, just as words for toilet, stomach etc. change in acceptability and

Doves in the Rat Race

euphemisms abound. How many people who are said to sleep together do much sleeping? Conventions on language are largely social conventions and the question arises as to whether there is any distinctive Christian position on all this. After all, we all need escape mechanisms sometimes and it could be that turning the air blue is a relatively harmless form.

The starting point for Christians has to be that some people find this sort of language hurtful and offensive. We need to be sensitive to them, because as Christians we are not in the business of offending or hurting people if it can possibly be avoided. Moreover the question must be raised as to whether swearing is not itself a form of violence because of the brutality of its worst forms. If so, it cannot be religiously acceptable. Some of it, however, has an apparently religious thrust.

'Oh, my God!' has become relatively socially acceptable. I have heard preachers describe it as inarticulate prayer. To me personally, bending it that far sounds a bit like 'creative accounting'. On the lips of Christians such a phrase seems disrespectful, to some blasphemous and inexcusably inarticulate as an approach to God. 'Christ!' is worse still and while as Christians we should use our God-given sense of humour and be ready to joke I hear echoes of 'taking my name in vain' too readily on this one to defend it as an expletive on Christian lips.

Christians are also expected to disapprove of soft porn. Again we need to recognize that for many it

Christian Behaviour

is distasteful, though it is strange that what is acceptable socially in the pages of some of our tabloid national daily newspapers is somehow thought of as unacceptable when it is produced with better quality photos in magazines that clearly warn about the contents and cannot be sold to minors. Is it likely to deprave and corrupt? Is it exploitation of women? Is it the selling of sexuality that is so offensive? Again, we need to have our own answers to these questions, for sooner or later at school or at work a copy will come our way and our peers will be watching for our response.

One pity, however, is that the crusade against soft porn diverts us so often from what I passionately believe as a Christian to be more harmful and that is the pornography of violence. Here, in glossy magazines and comics, on TV and in some books, violence is portrayed as exciting, glamorous, macho. Life, of the enemy, is of little account. They exist to be 'taken out'; they are not human at all. Unlike soft porn, there are no age limits to much of this stuff and infants can be bought comics and guns to match which reflect all these sorts of values. You can have the latest rocket attack vehicle for Christmas, the season of peace and goodwill. The reality is that violence is humiliating and life-threatening. Under systematic violence people can be crushed and their spirit destroyed. Yet we package it with no warning on the label! Violence can ruin your health and to sell suffering seems as bad, if not worse, than selling sex.

So if we are looking at things in society at which

Doves in the Rat Race

to protest many Christians will draw attention to areas that may not even be perceived by others to be problems or social issues at all. Attitudes to animals is one instance where our love for pets is strangely offset by our treatment of millions of other animals bred for the table. To other Christians the exploitation of workers in developing countries by companies that pay starvation wages is seen as of vital importance, even if the consequence of a fair wage for them would be to put our prices up. And do Christians who oppose the evils of alcohol also oppose the evils of smoking? For research on secondary smoking, i.e. smoke inhaled by non-smokers, suggests that if you persist in smoking you aren't just killing yourself any more, you're taking me with you if I have the misfortune to spend time with you in the room where you smoke. Yet smoking has received far less Christian social testimony than alcohol.

The important principle in all this is that if we are not careful society will decide what the risky sinful things are and then watch our reaction: alcohol, bad language etc. But society should not set the agenda for Christians and we should never be diverted from watching out for greater dangers that may be surrounding us unnoticed.

Dealing with the world in these areas is not the full extent of the dilemma. There is the whole question of our commitment to the world via career, ambition, promotion and the acquisition of material possessions. 'Live simply that others may simply live.' This is an excellent maxim to sum up

Christian Behaviour

what a Christian ought to do, but I am typing it on a word processor. Possibly that is one of many inconsistencies we all share on this issue. The breakaway Quaker group at Fritchley in Derbyshire put it in their 1924 Advices like this: 'Friends are advised to avoid superfluity in their manner of living, in dress, and in the furniture of their houses.' It is easy to preach renunciation to others, but it is a hard DIY lesson. We will always want to add that little bit more for ourselves. Or for our children. Second TV? Fine. Video? Yes. Second car? Perhaps. A more modern computer? OK. We are good at inventing 'needs'. The desire to be up-to-date coupled with our 'need' of the new item and a bit of old-fashioned covetousness can be quite overpowering. Each of the items we may fancy could be defensible, but when does their cumulative effect start to bite in a world where people starve? Still worse, confident that no formula could ever be agreed on to limit our possessions, because of all the exceptions that would have to be made, we can go on adding to our personal collections. In the tension of balancing need versus greed it is easy to give in. What does God think of all this? We console ourselves that no one can answer that question definitively. How glad we are. Jesus' teaching on wealth? 'It is easier for a camel to go through the eye of a needle than for a rich man to enter the Kingdom of God' (Mark 10.25). Well, we need to remember he lived in different times, his teaching needs re-interpreting and what would happen if we all gave our money

Doves in the Rat Race

away? With these and like sentiments we dodge the issue.

One way out of this is a self-imposed tax, 33% of my overtime, or whatever, to Christian Aid, so that when I am working extra hard for myself, I am also working for the poor. The more I achieve to reward myself, the more I feed them. So the taxman has his share, the charity has a third and I have the rest. Not too high a price, especially if I'm on double time.

As to choice of job itself it may be that some occupations are hard to square with the Christian faith: prostitution – though Jesus befriended prostitutes; volunteer soldiers, who could be called upon to kill; the munitions trade where, once your products are sold you lose control over their use; the tobacco industry whose products harm their consumers and others. There are other jobs that could be said to contribute to the loss of life or health.

But career isn't simply about the choice of job. It is also about how high up the ladder one goes. This in turn usually depends on that fine balance between personal choice, the ability to reach the next rung up the ladder and the chance factors in the selection process. It is so often assumed, however, that any person in his or her right mind will aim to go as high as possible. That is not a Christian assumption. The question is, how much time would the next level up allow for our family, for recreation, for worship and reflection? It may be right to stop now. When we are short of time in

Christian Behaviour

our present post we need to ask which of these areas – family, recreation, worship – is being pushed out and whether that is a right ordering of our lives.

Christians need also to question the common assumptions about a 'good job'. A good job is so often seen as a well-paid job, with prospects of promotion. Like all parents, Christian parents jealously guard their children in 14+ option choices in secondary school. They want them to choose well. How willingly they let them opt out of RE, a proper academic, employable subject, apart from the light it sheds on faith. How dismayed some churchgoing Christians are if their daughter or son shows an interest in full-time Christian ministry. To be paid a pittance! Unsocial hours! Twenty-four hour call! That's taking it too far ... Why not look at accountancy instead? Our attitude as Christians to career can be extremely revealing as a mirror reflecting our spirituality.

So living in the world will inevitably provide times of testing for our faith. Practising Christians are a minority group. The boss, the secretaries, our schoolmates, our daily circle of contacts will provide critical spectators. We may never satisfy them. We will never satisfy any standard of perfection, except perhaps perfection of intention, but we may have offered a witness based on integrity and conviction. In the materialistic and sometimes very unChristian society in which we live we shall have tried to live out the faith thoughtfully in our own orbit. I think we'll get some marks for that!

4 · TRYING TO BRING ABOUT A BETTER WORLD

Because of Jesus' command that Christians should love their neighbours as themselves, itself of course a repetition of the Jewish commandment, Christians have a long history of involvement to improve the lot of their fellow human beings. Although the Bible did not explicitly condemn slavery, the Christian conscience began to see it as an affront to the dignity of man whom the Bible certainly does proclaim to be God's creature and in God's image. So it was an essentially Christian witness that began to rise against it. Or again in the matter of penal reform it was the pressure of Quaker Christians in the UK, many of whom had personal experience of imprisonment on the pretext of their refusal to swear oaths (Matt. 5.33–37), that led to a push against the most barbarous excesses. It has been consistently true in this century that Christians have tried to reduce global suffering.

Although we may look in vain for an organization calling itself Christians For a Fairer Society

Christian Behaviour

or some more trendy mnemonic, very many Christians are nevertheless deeply involved in the work of Oxfam, Shelter, Amnesty International, the Campaign For Nuclear Disarmament, Samaritans, Marriage Guidance etc. A study of some of the leading officials in these organizations would reveal a Christian connection, sometimes ordination, for some of them. So while none of these groups is a specifically religious group, and atheists are and would be just as welcome in their leadership and ranks, we should not be surprised to find Christians very actively involved.

Perhaps this is one behavioural consequence of Christian belief; one cannot sincerely believe in the love of God and do nothing to help the starving. Inaction on the second would turn the first into a cruel lie. It is not always through charities either that Christians would seek this involvement; it may come through prison visiting or hospital visiting or some other social activity of this sort. It is also through the concerns of some of these groups such as Friends of the Earth or Greenpeace or Transport 2000 that Christian concern for the environment, which can be traced back all the way to Genesis 1, is found. This is stewardship of the planet which, the Bible reminds us constantly, is our responsibility and a service to the people who are to come.

Practicality restricts the amount of time each individual Christian has to spend on these activities, but if we were in search of the proverbial rule of thumb we could say that Christians ought to set aside time to be active in one or two of these groups

Doves in the Rat Race

and perhaps a sleeping partner (contributing mainly financially rather than in time) to several more. For the retired Christian there is opportunity to do more and it would certainly be sad in our world if any retired Christian felt on the scrap heap when so much help is needed in so many different areas that there must be outlets for everyone's talents. For the unemployed Christian the challenge is greater and perhaps the churches could increase their input to help the unemployed by providing travel costs and basic funds to enable some of them to be active in helping these organizations.

At this point the tinsel and the glitter end and the harder and more complex reality begins to emerge. Not all of these organizations are popular and some of them have been tarnished with a distinct political image. This may be because in different ways each of these groups is committed to change; change in the world's economies to discriminate in favour of the poor; change in our spending on weapons and reliance on threats to keep peace; change in the way we are treating or mistreating the planet; change so that the poor do have more, which one cannot deny must mean cuts somewhere else to give them the 'more'. The happy amateur jangling a collection tin on a flag day is thus transposed into someone who is very much criticizing things as they are and asking us to pledge ourselves, even by only 10p, to things as they might become.

Any system under criticism in this way will respond. It may pillory the people involved as left-wing or right-wing stirrers, according to the

Christian Behaviour

complexion of the establishment they are stirring against. It may attempt to coat them with a smear of unpatriotism. It may demand that the religious go back to their proper domain, the realm of the spirit, and stay well out of 'politics', which usually means in this context, trying to alter what suits me. Coupled with this is, of course, a real danger that some reformers will espouse a particular party political view of the issue they are concerned with and ride that bandwaggon – at their peril. When Christians go in quest of power to change the rules there is always the risk that the gospel of the powerless Christ will be left behind.

But the persuasion of Christians that they should become concerned with the realm of the spirit, with prayer, with doctrine, with Bible study etc., was what helped Hitler to come to power. He took the view that the churches were 'dynamite' (he used that word) but if they could be coaxed away from society and into the realm of the heavenly they would be tamed. And so Hell became a reality for Jews, gypsies, Jehovah's Witnesses, and the other inmates of the camps. Those Christians who want the church never to speak out on social issues must remember that this is where it led once and could do again. For the Germans were no guiltier in allowing this than the Jews were in allowing the execution of Jesus, or any nation is when decent people 'mind their own business' and evil is allowed to thrive. They were simply exhibiting human traits that are in all of us: the desire to get on with living and leave the wider scene to others; the

Doves in the Rat Race

failure to see the creeping advances of evil until too late; the refusal to see behind the moral pretensions of Hitler and an uncritical willingness to accept his moral puritan ticket – tougher punishment for criminals etc. . . our own passion for good order, security.

Another change since World War II that has made it now a necessity for Christians to be involved in social and political issues has been the gradual politicization of almost every department of human existence. By this I mean that all the great issues are now seen as political. Education is no longer seen as something the professional teachers know best about and should control; it is the politicians who pay on behalf of us all and have taken the reins not just of finance but of curriculum and policy. The days of the dictator headteacher, by no means a golden age, are over. The health service, another area which a generation ago was not seen as political, is now the subject of political controversy as politicians search for value for money or whatever. It is the political parties who have jumped on to the ground of the churches, not the reverse. Read any manifesto. It is a vision of the sort of society that party would like to see and how it will get us there, with the help of our vote. The Bible is full of visions about better societies and so should Christians be if they are serious about God's kingdom on earth. So Christians should not allow themselves to be ordered off the scene by politicians, for Christians have a higher allegiance than party or even state; conversely they must allow that

Christian Behaviour

in the present climate, politicians are going to involve themselves in all sorts of social and moral issues. There are bound to be clashes. But then slavery wasn't abolished overnight either; there was the strong political and economic argument that without a large pool of free labour there would be economic collapse, an argument which was revived to justify working children for long hours in appalling conditions in nineteenth-century factories.

So involvement in these issues may mean that Christians feel tainted with the label political and wounded in the cut and thrust of debate. What matters is that the Christian looks to God and not a party view for the vision. The legislative process may be a necessary part and it is important that just as politicians should not brand Christians 'political' (a strange insult from them!) Christians should not view politicians as a bunch of time-serving, power-mad semi-crooks. If one is to take an issue like abortion, which is a highly emotive subject on which most Christians have a view, even if Christians collectively disagree, there can be no change in what is happening except through the legislative process, whether the change is to ban abortion or tighten it up or make it easier to obtain. So many other issues are similar: defence, the health service, how much of the national product is given to Third World countries and on what terms. We have to talk to the politicians. Nor must we forget that some of them are Christians too!

Whether in the process of these attempts to bring

Doves in the Rat Race

about a more just and peaceful world we get called names doesn't matter. Jesus was called a glutton because he went to parties. John the Baptist was called a spoilsport because he didn't. You can't win! But in the famous parable the one talent man lost all he had, not for not winning, but for not trying (Matt. 25.24–30). Better to do what we believe to be right, always being ready to question and reconsider, and let God do any winning to be done.

PART FOUR
Christians Together

1 · AT WORSHIP

For many people outside or on the fringe of Christianity possibly the hardest dimension to understand is that of worship. I can sympathize strongly with this because it is of the nature of worship that it is self-authenticating. In other words if it works for you it is its own proof, but not the sort of proof that you can pass on to me so that I can be guaranteed to make it work. To the onlooker worship may understandably appear to be a meaningless ritual or empty charade. It may be that childhood has left an indelible impression on us. We may have grown up thinking of worship as a 999 call to God, only if you need it, a cry for help but not a conversation. Childhood church visits or primary school assemblies may have given the impression that prayer is simply talking to God. 'Hands together, eyes closed.' That ignores the listening aspect of prayer, which must matter, for if prayer were only talking, God would presumably know what we were going to say before we said it and therefore there would be no point in saying it, except to get something off our chest. Talking to the mirror would achieve that.

Doves in the Rat Race

Some people feel guilty that they get more out of sitting in an empty church building, or from the piece the organist plays before the service starts, than they do from the service itself. Perhaps we have too readily assumed that 'the service' is the only route to God and that no other aspect of life constitutes worship. That assumption has the effect of divorcing worship from life for 'the service' then becomes something unrelated and separate. We need to develop more the idea that the service can be the focal point of the week's worship. It can draw together strands in one's private or individual worship and provide thoughts and stimulus for the week ahead. When it works, that is.

The problem many people experience in organized worship is that they feel relegated to spectator status, in which they get up and down to sing hymns (the interludes) but basically have to sit and listen to the prayers, readings and sermon. In these days where radio is often used merely as a background noise, people find listening a demanding and draining activity. In fact they switch off! Most churches are well aware of these problems and seek to involve members of the congregation much more: in 'passing the peace', with the use of visual aids, in carefully planned family worship, moving preachers out of pulpits and down to earth, in simply using more people in leading worship so that a variety of faces and voices is common. It is harder to change the inbuilt attitude of some members, however, who still criticize the show at the end! 'It was a good preacher this morning.' 'I

Christians Together

didn't like the sermon,' and other similar remarks from the world of entertainment which imply that the role of the vicar or preacher is to please me.

If we are looking for analogy then formal worship can be seen as a play or drama, but not with us as uninvolved spectators but as actors, each with a part. The communion service, for example, can be interpreted as a solemn re-enactment of the Last Supper. By reading words from the Gospel accounts, by symbolic actions on the part of the priest or minister and the people, we re-create our sense of the mystery and deep meaning of this event. In a 'set' service the congregation have a script so that they can follow the events and play their part. The aim is not acting in the sense of pretending but acting in the sense of re-living or re-creating. It is proclamation: '... Every time you eat this bread and drink this cup you proclaim the Lord's death until he comes' (I Cor. 11.26). In this way we are encouraged to feel the meaning of the Last Supper rather than intellectualize it or appreciate it merely rationally.

Perhaps all this has still not penetrated what worship is. I see it as nothing less than communion with God. No more and no less. Formal worship is intended to help to bring that about, though formal worship cannot be the communion, it can only lead us into it. It is a communion not of bread and wine and outward symbols but of spiritual (and therefore deeply real) meeting. Almost, as it were, an intermingling of our selves and God. Bread and wine may lead us into that, but they are not the

Doves in the Rat Race

communion; they are its aids. We must therefore approach worship, in the old Quaker phrase, 'with heart and mind prepared', expecting this momentous possibility. If we are let down and don't feel this sensation of encounter with God we have to ask whether the failure lies in those presiding over the worship who should, as it were, have been midwives to this experience, or whether the failure lay in the form of worship used or whether the failure lay in our own unpreparedness or laziness of approach.

Singing hymns, eating bread, drinking wine, hearing Bible readings and sermons, embracing those around us, times of silence, matter only as far as they bring us into a fuller sense of God's presence. For while God is present at all times and in all places our degree of willingness or tuned-in-ness to receive him varies. Formal worship attempts, like turning the microscope lens, to focus and point up what is there potentially for us all the time.

So some will sense God most vividly in the act of eating the bread, or in the silence that follows receiving bread and wine; for others group meditative prayer will seem to bring God near. For others it may be as they are 'caught' by a phrase from the line of a hymn or from the words of a preacher. These are moments of awe, in which our busy-ness is stopped. That is what makes formal worship worthwhile and what we take away with us when the 'act of worship' ends. But God is not a vending machine. We can't put a coin in and expect refreshment at a particular time, in a particular

Christians Together

wa. He is not manipulated by our 'service' and the experience of communion will not come to all, nor will it always come. Nothing can be assumed. There is no sure magic formula to bring God near. He is not at our command. So worship always has that of risk, that of the unexpected about it, and the greatest saints testify that it can be a dreary experience at times. With such variable factors as ourselves involved this is hardly surprising. The relationship with God has this in common with a human relationship, that however well you think you know your partner, he or she will sometimes surprise you.

This element of the unexpected in planned formal worship applies more so outside it. In any situation we may feel suddenly close to God, or that God has come close to us: in an empty church; in flower gazing (Matt. 6.29); in sunshine seen through trees; on an open sea; when we witness birth or death; in an unsolicited kind remark to us; in a child's eyes; in the unexpected visitor who breaks our loneliness to see if we are 'all right'; in laughter between friends; when a conversation falls into a gathered silence; in lingering over a meal; in a precious memory ... In ten thousand thousand ways we may encounter God or he may, as it were, find us. The whole universe is potentially a place of worship and our response the anthem, albeit croakingly rendered.

Caught off guard in these sorts of ways we may experience a communion as deep as that in any formal worship. Like happiness, such experiences

Doves in the Rat Race

cannot be engineered. They are given and we have to accept them with joy (Mark 10.15). There is a danger in thinking that it is an either-or between these experiences and formal worship. Either we go to formal worship or we leave it to chance, to Providence or whatever. It should be both, for each experience feeds the other. We have to be awake and listening, however, to catch the voice within wherever we may be. Worship is work, not a cosy introspective dose. It is said that some arise strengthened after a sermon, while others awake refreshed.

These unplanned encounters with God are not regular or predictable. They are the good times in the life of the spirit, but the desert is part of that life as well. Here, at times of a spiritual dry patch, we may feel depressed, even despairing. At such times we ought always to pray, for prayer is the first step towards God. Prayer need never ask for a list of things, for the only thing God gives is himself. That is enough. All we can offer is our sense of need at a bad time. And when the clouds obscure even prayer, we have to remember that the desert and being deserted was part of Jesus' life. His friends left him (Mark 14.50). He could not feel God near (Mark 15.34). He felt abandoned. We know that at that time the whole thing seemed finished. But three days later and 2000 years later it is far from finished. No one gets out of a desert who sits down and gives in to despair. Even Jesus' cry of abandonment was a prayer: 'My God, my God, why did you abandon me?' We forget the 'My God' bit too easily.

2 · THE CHURCH

It may seem odd to put the church last in a book about Christian life-style, but the church is so vital to the subject and yet so misunderstood.

'Do you go to church?' is a very common question when people are discussing Christianity together, but how complex this simple question really is. For one thing, the question has no meaning unless the church is a building. Yet Christians have been quite clear for 2000 years that they belong not to a building but to a community, a common group of people. Indeed for the first 300 years, Christianity had no buildings, only the homes of its members to use for meetings. Even now everyone would agree that if the building burned down, there would still be a church. Moreover, house churches are actually reviving. All this means that the question we should be asking is not 'Do you go to church?' but 'Do you belong to the church?', for the church is a community, people, who are united in one astonishing claim. The claim is that in Christ and living in his spirit wealth, age, colour, race, sex, social class,

Doves in the Rat Race

job, IQ, whom you know, how bad your past life has been, none of these matter. It is revolutionary. No wonder some of the first Christians felt they had been born again. It is a call not essentially to a set of beliefs, but to a new way of living and loving, based on the life, death and return again of Jesus.

Cynical onlookers may reply, with evidence, that the church doesn't look very much like that. Of course there is truth in this, for it is a becoming community, an on-the-way community, a community of disciples (the Greek word means students) helping each other along. Who said birth wasn't painful! In any case judgmental onlookers, who assume that they're so much better than these poor failed Christians, have failed themselves in one of the first signs of the community and that is not to sit in judgment on other people but to leave that to God to sort out. He's had more experience and will make a better job of it. And he's got more of a sense of humour and mercy in dealing with folk than the hard line Christians or non-Christians who are so ready to write their opponents off.

But the complexity of the issue still isn't solved because some people wonder where the church is when they can only see churches, the denominations as they are sometimes called. It is true that most people arrive at their denomination by accident; they were brought up in it, or it was the nearest church to where they live or they heard there was a lively family service to take their children to when they moved into the area.

Christians Together

Provided the denominations are not exclusive, saying 'We're right and all the others are wrong', or even 'We're better than all the others', there is no shame in there being reasons almost of accident about which one you belong to.

The separate churches in reality worship and work together increasingly, though of course there remain churches who won't join any of the denominations (thus they become denominations of one) and some refuse to join in ecumenical worship because they're often busy erecting doctrinal barriers to keep the others out. If the others can't accept this, then we can't accept them etc. All this is a sign of fear. Perhaps it is the fear of takeover. Protestants once feared the Big Daddy of Rome; Roman Catholics once resented the breakaway heretics, whose clergy were seen as not proper clergy at all. Times are changing. What is on the scene is not the one, organizationally united church (PLC!) which will impose its pattern of ministry and its way of worship on all congregations, closing the little village chapel that we might like as it goes its mammoth way, a church which has to be run centrally because of its size. People have given up thinking that sort of church is desirable or possible. I'm sure if it arrived some group would fairly soon pick a quarrel and drop out. Christians are instead learning to share and to worship together at local level and when unity does come, if it comes, it comes because that is what the local people want; no one has taken them over. It was this real fear which led some to oppose the

Doves in the Rat Race

Anglican–Methodist unity scheme of 1964. It may have been similar fears that led some of the small Congregational chapels to decline to join the United Reformed Church when it was formed in 1972.

What the denominations offer most usefully, however, are different ways of worship and different ways of organizing Christians together. If we compare the Roman Catholic Mass with the average Methodist chapel service, the silent Quaker Meeting, the Salvation Army Meeting with band and songsters and the Pentecostal service with people leaping to their feet to praise God, we may conclude rightly that Christians will never want to worship in one way. They are far too varied a group of people for that. Different styles of worship will meet their varied individual needs. In the end the justification for joining one denomination rather than another is that the worship helps me to encounter God, which is what worship is really supposed to be all about. Any act of worship is useful as far as it helps me to do that. We all benefit, however, from sharing someone else's worship from time to time. It can enrich our understanding of the fullness of Christianity. It can give us new things to think about that we didn't notice in our own familiar, comfortable routines. It can even make us appreciate what is good in our own way of worship. What we should always be discouraging in the Christian faith is the ostrich approach which ignores those Christians whose interpretation of worship or doctrine or how the

Christians Together

church should be organized and run is different from our own.

Christianity is not about the little community that meets down the road in isolation from the rest of the Christian world. It is an international, multi-racial jigsaw in which the little community that meets down the road is one piece. Even within itself, it is not about resisting change. We reject the monolithic single corporation model of one united church; but we may have to disband the remnants of a dying or dead Christian community in one place (and close the building) in order to breathe new life into another somewhere else. God is no respecter of places. Ever since he moved Abram hundreds of miles (Gen. 12) Jews and Christians have understood that God is not stationary, nor should his people be. It is not without significance that whatever the guides tell us when we visit holy land sites, no single place connected with Jesus can now be shown to us, not in the sense of the exact spot. There are at least two crucifixion sites and a lot of inspired, or less inspired guesses about the other places in the life of Jesus. For the Christian conviction about Jesus has been that 'He is not here but risen.' There are many people, however, who are fond of saying 'I am a Christian but I don't go to church.' They sometimes go on to produce a whole string of rather lame and guilty excuses, like they didn't like the vicar or the services were boring (they didn't try another church!) or they could worship in the open air alone (but did they bother?). Despite what seem to be pretty feeble

Doves in the Rat Race

excuses, sometimes hotly and guiltily argued by some of these people, who must feel them to be inadequate since they defend them even before a word of comment has been uttered, I'm not going to fall into the trap of judging them and declaring roundly that they are not Christians and that they have deluded themselves and why don't they go to church next Sunday because ...

It is not for me to say they cannot be Christian. But it does seem clear, however, that to be a Christian on your own, without the help of an organization or group, is going to be much harder and call for more self-discipline.

Do the people who fall into this category bother to worship or pray or read the Bible or involve themselves in some of the organizations we have discussed as part of their individual Christianity? Or is it really what the sceptics would call a vague insurance policy? They like the cover, but without the premium, so that if an Act of God occurs they can claim they are on the right side. I don't know! I do know that the limited sample I've met don't seem to translate the assertion that they are Christian into any real quantifiable action or belief. Ones I haven't met may do.

In contrast to this view the New Testament talks a lot about the New Israel, a Christian community. It doesn't say much about individual, i.e. separate Christians. Perhaps the analogy in the end is political. A person could claim to be a socialist. Under pressure they could point out that they believed in socialist dogma, fair shares for all etc.

Christians Together

But if asked why they hadn't joined the local Labour Party to help to bring a socialist government into power, to put into practice socialist principles, why they hadn't canvassed and leafletted at election time, why they hadn't even sent a donation, they would remain unconvincing, if the reply was that although they did none of these things they did think about socialism carefully and sincerely when out walking along the canal bank. How different is being a Christian from this parallel?

Within the church community, however, Christ is central to its worship and work. He is at the heart of the experience though we may use different words to describe his effect on us and to try to think out the meaning of his life. He impels us to create a more loving world and to take out the community as we see it can be in Christ, into the community of the villages and cities in which we live and into the global community. We carry the hope within the Christian community that love never ends and because of this as a community can stand against death itself, maintaining it to be like the experience of passing through a waterfall into new existence with fuller communion with God. When our worship is at its deepest and best we see the curtains part, fleetingly, and in the preached word or the communion wafer or the still silence we glimpse that eternity which preachers preach and poets dream of; we glimpse the past and future of our community ... and then the veil descends again, the act of worship rumbles on. We clutch a

Doves in the Rat Race

fragment of a vision to take home with us after the closing prayer.

As a community we are aware that our faith as individuals is weak and needs to be nurtured and built up. We have a lot to learn from one another and the study group sessions are second only in importance to the worship in the development of our spiritual life, along with our care for one another, which we then extend into our social and moral and global concerns. For the pure motive will always be care for others and not power over them. Perhaps we shall check our own career progress in order to leave time for all this to be done, content with less than the highest job of which we are capable in order to leave time for the family and for the Christian community and for worship of God.

Deciding whether to join this community does not mean waiting for certainty, for a voice from heaven that ends all doubts and solves all questions. It doesn't mean being able to tick next to a doctrinal checklist what you believe and if you get the jackpot, you're in. Still less does it mean throwing ourselves into so many good works and committees that our family life is neglected and our spiritual life is destroyed. Protect the church from do-gooders! The real call, the unsettling call, through the voice that crosses the centuries, is a very simple one. It is the call to drop the nets of our self-pre-occupation and try to follow Christ in a spirit of Christ-like love.

Acknowledgments

Unless otherwise stated, all scripture quotations are from the Good News Bible (British usage edition), published by the Bible Societies and Collins, © American Bible Society 1966, 1971, 1976. Reproduced by permission.

The extract from William Penn (1693) quoted in the section about the next world is reproduced by kind permission of the Quaker Home Service for the Religious Society of Friends from their spiritual anthology *Christian Faith and Practice in the Experience of the Society of Friends*, published by London Yearly Meeting, 1960.

John Stacey of the Epworth Press added his own encouragement to the writing, by his manner as well as his words, for which I am grateful.

I was brought up as a Christian and owe many of my insights to others. Few thoughts in the world on any issue must be truly original. I owe a lot to many Christians I have met or read. Being brought up as a Christian, however, or reading about it, isn't enough. You have to make the faith your own. No one else can do it for you. Yet,

Doves in the Rat Race

paradoxically, we are never alone. I owe a real debt to my Copley grandparents, parents, wife and children; to a Methodist upbringing that taught me that great-heartedness is a more important test of Christian living than doctrine and to Friends (Quakers) from whom I learnt how to listen to God and what prayer is.